PROCESS CONSULTING

PROCESS CONSULTING

How to Launch, Implement, and Conclude
Successful Consulting Projects

*Powerful Techniques
for the Successful Practitioner*

ALAN WEISS, Ph.D.

Author, *The Ultimate Consultant*

JOSSEY-BASS/PFEIFFER
A Wiley Company
www.pfeiffer.com

The ULTIMATE
CONSULTANT
Series

Published by Pfeiffer
A Wiley Imprint
989 Market Street, San Francisco, CA 94103-1741   www.pfeiffer.com

ISBN: 0-7879-5512-4

Pfeiffer books and products are available through most bookstores. To contact Pfeiffer directly call our Customer Care Department within the U.S. at 800-956-7739, outside the U.S. at 317-572-3986, or fax 317-572-4002.

Pfeiffer also publishes its books in a variety of electronic formats. Some content that appears in print may not be available in electronic books.

Acquiring Editor: Matt Davis
Director of Development: Kathleen Dolan Davies
Development Editor: Leslie Stephen
Editor: Rebecca Taff
Senior Production Editor: Dawn Kilgore
Manufacturing Supervisor: Becky Carreño
Interior Design: Gene Crofts
Illustrations: Lotus Art

Library of Congress Cataloging-in-Publication Data

Weiss, Alan, date
  Process consulting : how to launch, implement, and conclude successful
consulting projects : powerful techniques for the successful
practitioner / Alan Weiss.
      p. cm.
Includes bibliographical references and index.
  ISBN 0-7879-5512-4
  1. Business consultants. I. Title.
  HD69.C6 W463 2002
  001—dc21   2002004445

Printed in the United States of America

Printing 10 9 8 7 6 5

For Trotsky,
the Wonder Dog

Also by ALAN WEISS

Books

The Ultimate Consultant Series:

How to Acquire Clients (2002)
Value-Based Fees: How to Charge—and Get—What You're Worth (2002)
How to Establish a Unique Brand in the Consulting Profession (2001)
The Ultimate Consultant (2001)

How to Sell New Business and Expand Existing Business in Professional Service Firms (2001)
Getting Started in Consulting (2000)
The Unofficial Guide to Power Management (2000)
How to Market, Establish a Brand, and Sell Professional Services (2000)
Good Enough Isn't Enough (1999)
How to Write a Proposal That's Accepted Every Time (1999)
Money Talks (1998)
Million Dollar Consulting (1992; rev. ed. 1998, 2002)
Our Emperors Have No Clothes (1995)
Best Laid Plans (1991)
Managing for Peak Performance (1990)
The Innovation Formula (with Mike Robert, 1988)

Booklets

How to Maximize Fees
Raising the Bar
Leadership Every Day
Doing Well by Doing Right
Rejoicing in Diversity

Audiocassettes

Peak Performance
The Consultant's Treasury
The Odd Couple®

Videos

Stories I Could Never Tell: Alan Weiss Live and Uncensored
Alan Weiss on Marketing
Alan Weiss on Product Development

Newsletters

Balancing Act: Blending Life, Work, and Relationships (electronic)
The Consultant's Craft
What's Working in Consulting (editor)

About the Author

Alan Weiss began his own consulting firm, Summit Consulting Group, Inc., out of his home in 1985 after being fired by a boss with whom he shared a mutual antipathy. Today, he still works out of his home, having traveled to fifty-one countries and forty-nine states, published twenty books and over four hundred articles, and consulted with some of the great organizations in the world, developing a seven-figure practice in the process.

His clients have included Merck, Hewlett-Packard, Federal Reserve Bank, State Street Corp., Fleet Bank, Coldwell Banker, Merrill Lynch, American Press Institute, Chase, Mercedes-Benz, GE, American Institute of Architects, and over two hundred similar organizations. He delivers fifty keynote speeches a year and is one of the stars of the lecture circuit. He appears frequently in the media to discuss issues pertaining to productivity and performance and has been featured in teleconferences, video conferences, and Internet conferences.

His Ph.D. is in organizational psychology, and he has served as a visiting faculty member at Case Western Reserve, St. John's, and half a dozen other major universities. He currently holds an appointment as adjunct professor at the graduate school of business at the University of Rhode Island, where he teaches a highly popular course on advanced consulting skills. His books have been translated into German, Italian, and Chinese.

The New York Post has called him "one of the most highly regarded independent consultants in the country," and *Success Magazine,* in an editorial devoted to his work, cited him as "a worldwide expert in executive education."

Dr. Weiss resides with his wife of thirty-three years, Maria, in East Greenwich, RI.

Contents

Introduction

This is the first book of the twenty or so I've written which focuses exclusively on the implementation of consulting methodology. That's an elaborate way of saying, "Here's how you work with a client." This is not rocket science. It's something much more difficult—common sense. You'll find that my approach to virtually every consulting intervention is simple, non-convoluted, and relatively fast. That's why they are "ultimate" in my view: They are simple and effective.

Although I'll address specific interventions, I'm going to first focus on those issues which are much more important, and much less interesting, to most consultants: the need to effectively and relentlessly educate the buyer about, and prepare the environment for, the resources and focus required to support the project's implementation.

The finest of methodologies will be undone by a "lip service" buyer, an intransigently opposed senior executive, or an organizational immune system that rejects foreign bodies. The most average of techniques will succeed blazingly well when senior sponsorship is strong, rewards encourage participation, and self-interests are effectively accommodated. Once the sale is made, the implementation will rely *not on the skills of the consultant*, which I'll stipulate are probably excellent among the readers of this advanced series, *but rather on the volition and energy of the client* in assisting and supporting the implementation.

Doctors can't make patients take medicine or engage in exercise regimens, short of emergency measures. Consultants rarely have the opportunity to strap the client to a gurney and begin intravenous fluids. We require commitment, not mere compliance.

Consulting is not about something that we do to the client. It's about something that the client and we accomplish ensemble, one of us being unable to achieve that level of results without the partnership of the other. That applies to strategy formulation, focus groups, workshops, coaching, sales development, systems integration, outsourcing, and virtually any other consulting specialty.

My intent within these pages is to suggest how you can expediently and thoroughly prepare yourself, the buyer, and the client implementers to best accept and support your intervention. Then we'll talk about your alternatives to actually implement change.

But first, you have to be receptive to some change yourself.

Alan Weiss, Ph.D.
East Greenwich, RI
July 2002

Acknowledgments

I'd like to thank the wonderful editors and staff at Jossey-Bass/Pfeiffer, who have made this seven-book series one of the most enjoyable and pleasurable undertakings of my writing career. My appreciation particularly to Kathleen Dolan Davies, Matt Davis, and Matt Holt. Also my thanks to Leslie Stephen, who has diligently edited and improved each book in the series.

CHAPTER 1

Conditions for a Successful Intervention

Stacking the Deck in Consulting Is Not Cheating

Consulting techniques and interventions don't succeed or fail based on the atmosphere of the client, the self-esteem of the consultant, or the phase of the moon. They succeed or fail based, largely, on whether conditions conducive to their success or failure are in place.

The bad news is that is an implacable dynamic. The good news is that we control the dynamic, the client does not.

The reason that we've seen barely coherent approaches often triumphantly resound to the huzzahs of repeat business and the prized jewels of our beloved methodology fall to the ground and become lost amidst the macadam is that the *conditions* that obtain actually produce victory or defeat. Centuries ago Machiavelli wrote in *The Prince*, "I have often reflected that the causes of the successes or failures of men are dependent on their ability to suit their manner to the times."

How well can you massage, manage, and maneuver the environment so that your intervention is ideally suited to the conditions of the times?

Above all—and I hope this thought will resonate and carom throughout the book—we cannot afford the conceit of falling in love with our own methodologies. Our best six approaches to the sales process, strategy facilitation skills, conflict resolution technology, and assorted other proprietary (or simply beloved) approaches are not the point. They are merely means to an end, and that end had better be the improved condition of the buyer.

No buyer ever said, "Our people don't understand their roles in terms of our strategic intent any better than before, but that consultant had a fabulous nine-box grid, superb computerized reminder lists, and a wonderful facilitation technique." What that buyer says is, "Let's never do *that* again!" and "Is it too late to get our money back?"

EDUCATING THE BUYER

Prior to the sale you probably had to educate the buyer about need, value, metrics, and other aspects of your proposal.[1] However, that education doesn't end with the signed contract or the buyer's check clearing the bank. You must constantly educate the buyer about the needs, progress, and accountabilities of the consulting project. That begins with the first meetings when you're establishing a relationship and ends with . . . well, it never really ends.

Ultimata: Your methodology is not nearly as important as the client's *receptivity* to support methodology. If achieving the latter means modifying the former, then do so. The equation does not work in the other direction. The client will never love your methodology as much as you do!

---

1. See the other books in this series for the "pre-sale" education, especially *Value-Based Fees* and *How to Acquire Clients*. Also see my book *How to Write a Proposal That's Accepted Every Time* (Kennedy Information, 1999).

Here are the fundamental educational processes you should utilize during and after the sale to ensure the success of your implementation. It doesn't hurt to keep a physical checklist of these requirements so that you can ensure you don't skip a step or miss a beat.

Five-Step Client Education Checklist

1. Establish Crisp Objectives. Create very clear business outcomes for the project. Translate "inputs" (your methodology or the tasks required) into "outputs" (the improved client condition stated as business outcomes). Examples:

Input or Methodology	Business Result or Objective
Conduct focus groups	Determine employee commitment to new compensation plan
Facilitate strategic retreat	Create top-team consensus on nature and direction of the business
Serve as expert witness	Enable client to defend against lawsuit successfully
Coach general manager	Enable senior executive to delegate to subordinates, focus on acquisitions

Crisp objectives will also circumscribe the project, preventing the dread "scope creep," which afflicts many consulting interventions like a fungus growing out of control in the dark and moisture of vague agreements.

2. Establish Clear Accountabilities. A consulting project is not something you "do" to the client. It's something that the two of you mutually engage in—a collaboration or partnership requiring both of your talents, vantage points, and hard work. My proposals *always* include a section called "joint accountabilities," meaning that there are responsibilities uniquely mine, uniquely the buyer's, and uniquely shared by us. Examples:

Buyer: Make certain documents available, provide access to key people, visibly support the initiative at agreed on events and junctures, provide personal feedback, and so on.

Consultant: Provide periodic reports and updates, facilitate and manage all interventions as agreed on, adhere to confidentiality/non-compete agreements, and so forth.

Mutual: Inform each other immediately of anything learned that could materially affect the success of the project (e.g., the consultant learns that two key officers are resigning in the next month, or the buyer learns that there will be a major acquisition or divestiture).

Ultimata: The buyer knows about making cars, selling insurance, or creating brands on the Internet. You know about consulting. As you educate yourself about the buyer's business, why shouldn't the buyer be educated about yours?

---

3. Co-Opt Key Sponsors. Find the people who will make this project succeed or fail internally. Then cajole, romance, subvert, twist arms, and/or influence them in any way possible. These formal and informal sponsors are usually among the following:

- Buyer's direct reports
- Buyer's boss
- Key union officers
- Managers of key functions (e.g., sales)
- Top producers
- Key channel partners or agents
- Buyer's informal advisors
- Senior financial officers
- Large, influential customers
- Influential vendors

Enlist the buyer in helping you make the case to these people, always remembering that "What's in it for me?" will be their explicit or implicit question, and that question needs to be answered completely and satisfactorily.

4. Prepare the Buyer for Wins and Losses.   Every project I've ever been engaged in has had its share of false starts, setbacks, and "whoopses." Maybe that's because I'm just not that good. But maybe that's because such yin and yang are inevitable. If the latter is true, then you'd better prepare the buyer (and yourself).

Spell out for the buyer what may go wrong and why. For example:

- People who feel threatened will probably complain
- A lack of sponsorship will create doubts about sincerity
- The message will have to be repeatedly reinforced, not spoken just once accompanied by a banner in the cafeteria
- Senior people must "walk the talk"
- Unforeseen events will undoubtedly intervene, seldom for the better
- Eventually, there will be conflicting priorities to be resolved by the buyer

The more you can prepare the buyer for these eventualities, the better he or she will be able to see, even after the rose-colored glasses are discarded.

5. Make It Clear That Metrics Are Everything.   If the two of you aren't jointly measuring progress at frequent intervals, then no good can come of it. If things go poorly, the buyer will feel surprised and mistreated. If things go exceedingly well, the buyer will wonder if you really were needed at all.

Some metrics can be objective and some subjective. The key is that you and the buyer agree on how you'll measure progress, and you both agree that the measurement device is fair. Some examples:

Objective	*Subjective*
Weekly sales reports	Talking to salespeople and customers
Quarterly financial results	Monitoring the customer complaint line
Monthly turnover	Nature of grievances brought to HR
Customer retention	Customer feedback on support
Rejects and quality data	Vendors stop complaining

The best measure is one on which you and the buyer can agree, to quote Bob Mager's famous line, that you know it when you trip over it.

> *Ultimata:* Don't allow any buyer to stipulate, "I'll just know that we've achieved it." Despite the Supreme Court justice who said he'd know pornography when he saw it, consulting results are seldom so unequivocal or fascinating unless you specify what it is you're both looking for.

Educate the buyer in a manner that will be conducive to the success of your project. If you don't, no one else will, so you don't exactly have a lot of backup here.

MEETING KEY PLAYERS

Since the sales process can easily involve no one other than the buyer, it's important to spend some time on techniques required to meet and influence the key players described above. Remember that these are often people who will be threatened, indifferent, callused from prior experiences, cynical, sycophantic, and/or insincere.

Other than that, they're a fine bunch.

You must always keep the following absolute truth in mind when seeking to influence "key others": People will only willingly change their own behavior (motivation, as opposed to mere movement when ordered to change) when their own rational self-interest is affected. It is incumbent on you to identify, understand, and appeal to that rational self-interest.

> *Ultimata*: Consultants have no organizational power, and attempting to utilize the buyer's hierarchical power is cowardly (as well as ineffective). Determine and explain why it's best for others to change, not why it's best for you for them to change.

Dealing with the CEO of a $600 million subsidiary outside of Chicago, we agreed on a project to improve the collaboration and teamwork of his direct reports. The problem was that, as is so often the case, his "team" was really a committee. See Appendix A, Figure A.1, for a visual comparison of the two.[2]

"How would you know they have moved to true teamwork?" I asked, desperately seeking a metric.

"Oh, I'd just know," he assured me.

"Well, what's happening now that convinces you they aren't there yet?"

He listed the following:

- "They don't share resources.
- They argue over turf issues and who gets credit at my management meetings.
- I have to play referee constantly.
- Their own reports follow their lead and don't cooperate with their counterparts cross-functionally."

I simply reversed these and had fabulous metrics, for example, "If you no longer played referee at meetings or in your office, and they shared their resources and budgets as needed without you making the Solomon-like decision, then they would be a team."

"Yes," he said, "they would be a team and you would be a miracle worker." It turned out that he was right on both counts.

---

2. Appendix A is a compilation of many of my "process visuals," which I use to educate buyers and derive consensus from key players. For more examples and details on use, see my book *The Great Big Book of Process Visuals, or Give Me a Double Axis Chart and I Can Rule the World* (Summit Consulting Group, Inc., 2000).

Work with the buyer to determine who the key players are; then develop a plan *to influence every one of them positively.* This won't always work, of course. You'll have entrenched hard heads and purely personal agendas at work. But if you make the effort, you'll convert more than your share and tremendously soften the environment to accept the kind of interventions the client requires.

Here's a road map for identifying and influence key others.[3]

The Road Map to Influencing and Educating Key Others

1. Identify the Key Players Whose Support (or at Least Non-Opposition) You Require. The criteria can include

- Respected by large numbers of people
- Controls resources essential to the project
- Possesses expertise key to your successful implementation
- Has caused the success or failure of similar endeavors in the past
- Possesses or controls information key to implementation

There's nothing wrong with putting these criteria in front of the buyer and generating a list.

2. Set Priorities. Not everyone is equally important, and you don't have all the time or energy in the world. After all, the project has to begin before every duck is in a row and every cat has been taught to dance. Determine, with the buyer, who can absolutely derail the project, as opposed to those who can simply put sand on the track.

Begin with the derailers, and get to the sanders as time permits. Usually co-opting the former will drag along the latter.

3. Create a Tailored Plan for Each. Usually the worst thing you can do is to get everyone in a room and tell them what you're going to do for them, which will

---

3. Lest you think this is the buyer's sole responsibility and resides with the buyer as a result of my own "joint accountabilities," think again. The buyer has all kinds of political, cultural, ego, and turf constraints, which actually makes it easier for you to exert influence than for the buyer to do so in many cases.

make the IRS seem genuine and empathetic by comparison. Instead, devise a way to approach each based on self-interest. Which of them are anxious for new assignments, for new resources, for more freedom, for greater recognition, for healthier life balance, and so on?

Do your utmost to merge the buyer's business objectives with each individual's personal objectives. For example, if a given manager has long held that she's working too hard, demonstrate how the project will enable her to put in a forty-five-hour week and reach the same results she now achieves. If a union leader has qualms about losing control, show how the project's plan for delegation will actually push decisions to front-line levels.

Find out what makes them tick; then provide the fuel.

4. Keep Them in the Loop. The greatest consulting implementation sin I've encountered is keeping potential supporters in the dark, even after initially good meetings and budding relationships. Keep them aboard by

- Developing steering committees and advisory boards with their participation
- Copying them on reports, updates, and summaries sent to the buyer
- Inviting them to key buyer meetings
- Frequently asking for their suggestions, input, and critiques (it's far better to get a critique to your face than behind your back)

5. Establish and Monitor Their Accountabilities. Gain agreement from the buyer and the others about their involvement and responsibilities, and monitor the progress. In that way, you have frequent and regular excuses not only to interact, but to remind them of the support needed. *Hint:* The more specific the accountabilities, the harder they are to shirk or ignore.

Ultimata: Passion is a thin line between love and hate. If someone virulently opposes your project, finding his or her "hot button" (self-interest) will convert that zeal to your support. Remember that logic makes people think, but emotion makes them *act.*

Once upon a time, before the Messiah-like return of Steve Jobs, Apple Computer created an initiative to promote certain computer products zealously. The sales force dutifully complied—by low-balling their sales forecasts, attempting to ensure that they would maximize their bonuses by exceeding those same conservative forecasts.

Sales management dutifully complied—by knocking still more off the estimates, thereby preventing any overly zealous sales forecasts from preventing the sales managers from exceeding their goals for incentive pay.

Production dutifully complied—by creating an inventory completely consistent with the ghastly low sales estimates, and woefully inadequate for the actual demand once every salesperson and sales manager proceeded to burst through his or her incentive goal with unprecedented sales.

The result was a travesty, with Apple unable to meet orders, those orders being lost, and market share precipitously dropping. The CEO was canned, heads rolled, and Jobs returned.

Never doubt the efficacy of having the key implementers on board and communicating with all other key parties. Lack of such preparation nearly sank Apple, and it can surely sink you in any client system.

AVOIDING ENVIRONMENTAL AND POLITICAL LAND MINES

There are people opposed to any change in the status quo. The importance of recognizing and dealing with them is two-fold: First, they may undermine or deflect your project. Second, you may be receiving "false positives" from them if they are a resource for your information gathering (e.g., part of an interviewing process).

The first rule is to never assume that people are somehow "damaged." The myth that *all* people resist change simply isn't borne out by observing daily corporate reality: People adjust to traffic jams, unexpected management moves, customer unpredictability, power failures, and a myriad of other unexpected but clearly survivable potential detours to daily progress. People will change, but not all of them and not always readily.

> *Ultimata:* Don't mistake your own competence and chaste persona as the view that others will see. They will be biased by past experiences, company folklore, private interests, and bad hair days. Take active and aggressive steps to defuse land mines and win converts.

Here are the "likely suspects":

The Vested Interest

This individual truly has reason not to change. The current state of affairs maximized his or her well-being, and a comfortable nest is being threatened. An ideal example is the sales manager who sees the current compensation system as ideal both to effectively manage the salespeople and to squeeze every last penny out of his or her personal incentive bonus scheme.

You can deal with a vested interest in one of two ways:

1. Provide an Even Greater Interest. Demonstrate that your proposed change might lower the downside, but will greatly enhance the upside or will sacrifice some at-risk commissions while guaranteeing a larger monthly base. Vested interests often become locked into position because they haven't taken the time to look at alternatives once they get comfortable.

2. Clearly Show That It's to Be Either Supported Change or Uncontrolled Chaos. That is, the present condition is untenable, and they might as well work to create a new one that is most beneficial for them, or it will happen by default. If the compensation last year was 34 percent of revenues and 15 percent above industry averages, show that the system is going to change and no force in the world can stop that, since we're talking about irate shareholders and outraged executives. Given that inevitability, why don't we work together to create a tolerable new scenario?

The Conniver

The conniver has nothing against the change, per se, but sees an opportunity to barter or gain something in return for his or her support. This is the person holding Marvin Gardens in Monopoly™, preventing you from controlling all the yellow properties. In business, an example would be the IT manager who ingenuously claims that it would take months to change the sales reporting system to reflect new commission structures. Of course, she has also suggested that receiving frozen funding for new servers would greatly ease the burden.

Rule of Thumb: If the quid pro quo attempt is, indeed, for something that will materially assist in the implementation of the project, try to work it in. If it's a matter of crude ransom instead, then go to your buyer and relate this: "I have good news and bad news. We've cleared every obstacle to implementation but one. However, that one obstacle will require your direct clout to remove, since the issue is about corporate policy and funding."

Ultimata: You can't deal with all resistance in the same way. The *cause* of the resistance should dictate the preventive measures. The key is to be prepared for all of the types so that the preventive measures can be rapidly deployed. The cardinal sin—the fatal trap—is to allow resistance to undermine the buyer's belief in the project. Once that happens, the land mine has become a neutron bomb.

The Dilettante

Finally, you will sometimes encounter an intellectually gifted and interpersonally challenged manager who is adept at pointing out theoretical and conceptual "problems" which other managers—including your buyer—may react to with a combination of cautions and time-consuming attempts at preventive actions and counter-measures. His goal is nothing other than to demonstrate intellectual prowess, thereby safeguarding or improving a position as key advisor or heir apparent.

This can be the worst kind of resistance, since there is no clear opposing interest involved. In fact, it's rather like passive-aggressive behavior in that the resisting party is actually cloaking himself or herself in "the best interests of the project" by highlighting the "problems." You will usually have to overcome this person in a group meeting by employing the following techniques:

1. *Focus on probability and seriousness.* The conceptual claims usually will not stand up under pragmatic reality and, if actually encountered, can be easily overcome. So demonstrate that they are improbable and/or non-fatal, and show that the organization actually overcomes such issues every day in a variety of areas.
2. *Establish preventive and contingent actions quickly.* In other words, if the concern is that customers might react poorly if not brought into the loop well before your project is implemented and their feedback invited, suggest a rapid email or faxed customer survey and training of the sales force to deal with any customer reactions that are encountered on the spot. Show your buyer that there are actions immediately feasible that obviate the need for any delay.

The Cynical and Uninformed

Probably the greatest volume of resistance will come from the otherwise neutral folks who have seen (or think they've seen) a bushel of boondoggles before and who have no reason to suspect that this one will be any different. Those who are on the fence can be easily swayed by the skeptics.

Every project plan should have a strong communications aspect at the front end. Don't simply march through the building. Begin with some proper and moderate communications which alert the staff to the following:

- Why the project is important (the current condition to be improved)
- How you will be implementing the project
- What the results are hoped to provide
- What's in it for them
- How you will all know that progress is being made
- What recourse they have to ask questions and track that progress
- Who they might be encountering in that endeavor

Some projects demand confidentiality, but they are the minority. Let everyone know what's going on and you'll create an atmosphere of disclosure and trust rather than one of secrecy and cynicism.

WADING RIGHT IN: TEN STEPS TO LAUNCH

Despite my warning of possible land mines, I am strongly advocating that you "wade right in" to the project. I call this "throwing cement at the project," meaning that you want to get started, begin influencing the environment, become known, and get paid (most of all) before the resistance has a chance to erect fortifications.

The preventive measures above are meant to be naturally deployed in advance and/or as resistance is encountered. But the watchword is "forward."

Here are my guidelines for beginning the implementation of any project. You might choose to change the sequence, but I think the template will work over 90 percent of the time.

Ten Steps to Launch Without Being Sunk
1. *Reaffirm the proposal content with the buyer.* The buyer has signed your proposal or contract. As you begin the implementation, talk to the buyer to reaffirm what each of you is accountable for and how you're going to proceed from that point.

When beginning a project for what was once Merck's animal health division, I found that the focus group participants were virtually mute. Finally, I was told by someone, sotto voce, over coffee: "The sales director put the word out: He's picking us deliberately with the understanding that we won't say a negative thing about his leadership." How bad was his leadership? Well, he demanded that people give up a weekend night to attend "social functions" without their spouses so that he could enjoy the limelight.

I went to the division president and told him what was going on. He said he'd have a word with him. I cautioned against it. "Let me do random interviews around the division and pull together focus groups ad hoc at sites I visit without a schedule submitted through his office." We agreed on the plan and, in one rapid-fire week, I gathered all of the information I needed before the sales director could anticipate my next stop (he couldn't intimidate the entire division).

He later protested that I had "rigged" the damaging feedback and offered his own counter-testimonials about his behavior. It was then too late for him, but it had nearly been too late for me.

2. *Begin doing something.* The sooner you actually do something—anything—the quicker the client is committed and any chance for "cold feet" is defeated. Schedule some meetings, observe the work environment, meet key people, whatever it takes. But show immediate movement and create the momentum that will overcome the current inertia.

3. *Find and meet the key players.* As discussed above, there are influential people to meet and sway, either to support the cause or to prevent them from becoming resistance islands. Find them quickly. The reason is that it's hard to dislike someone who's taken the time to come to your office and ask your opinion, but it's relatively easy to dislike a "faceless" consultant being bad-mouthed by a colleague. Put a face behind your name and a firm handshake behind your introduction.

4. *Begin co-opting resistance.* Once you have a sense for where the resistance originates, implement the preventive and contingent actions noted above.

Don't assume it will dissipate through lack of energy or will be blunted by the mere force of your competence and commitment to the public weal. Fight them on the beaches.

5. *By-pass islands.* Having said that, don't get too bloody too early, and most critically, don't allow progress to slow because of islands of resistance. If the entire sales or financial department is resisting, that's one thing; but if a single financial manager is the naysayer despite her colleagues' support for you, then allow the skeptic to defend her island and flow around her. You can always come back later with reinforcements, but the odds are that, if you're successful, she will have been starved out. *The key here is forward motion. Don't allow minor resistance to stall your plans.*

6. *Periodically meet with the buyer.* A critical shortcoming of consultants is that they abandon the buyer.[4] Meet with the buyer every two weeks, at least, to demonstrate progress and discuss any obstacles. Problems are much more tolerable when confronted in the context of overall progress and victories. *Never* see the buyer only when you have problems to report. After the first couple of months, you may reduce the buyer contact to once a month, but that should depend on your own acceleration.

7. *Make your successes visible to the organization.* Use email, newsletters, house organ interviews, management meetings, and any other relevant mechanisms to ensure that the maximum number of people are acquainted with the progress. (The grapevine will surely be taking care of your problems and "defeats.") Cite clear examples, which will help eradicate those remaining islands of resistance. Also, embrace the internal people, which brings me to the next point.

8. *Share credit, or even bestow all of it.* The more you make the implementers responsible and the reason for success, the more you maximize your chances of everyone jumping on the bandwagon. The more the consultant is the sole wizard, the more you imply that "You were too stupid to get this done without me." Take a low-key role and accentuate the role of internal partners. Your support will grow like a fungus.

---

4. In larger firms, a "handoff" takes place, wherein the rainmaker (engagement manager) leaves and the implementation team takes over. That is a critical error, and one of the dumbest strategies that large firms employ.

I had begun a project for Mercedes-Benz North America and the CEO at the time was an extremely intimidating executive from the German parent. He was clearly unhappy with his human resource people, and I was brought in to do things that they were incapable of in his eyes.

At a social affair for dealers which introduced our initiative, several HR managers approached the CEO with some suggestions, which he peremptorily dismissed or abruptly cut off. He then turned to me and said, "What would you do?" I quickly answered him with hard facts and solid suggestions.

He said, "Perfect! Why can't you think like that?!"—the latter directed to the HR contingent. The tension was so high that I thought a fire might break out. But I calmly said, "Actually, several of those ideas were from your people, which we all shared just before this function."

"Ah," he muttered.

Later in the night, the vice president of human resources said, "Thank goodness you're here. You'll tell him things we've been trying to get across for two years, but he'll listen to you." It was a perfect marriage for the duration of the project.

9. *Illustrate closure.* When a portion of the project or a step in the plan is completed, blow the horn. Don't assume that everyone knows. Announce, diplomatically, that a key juncture has been reached.

Ultimata: Never lose the buyer's ear. Make arrangements early to meet frequently and on a schedule that is sacrosanct. If you ignore this, you deserve what you get, which will be very little.

10. *Visibly make mid-course corrections.* I've never been involved with a major project that played out exactly the way I had envisioned at the beginning. Don't hide redirection and regrouping. Let people know and explain why.

This is not a sign of weakness but a sign of strength. Be honest and people will trust you. Be secretive or disingenuous and people will suspect you're lying when you say, "Hello."

FINAL THOUGHT

Always make sure that you get PAID on time. This is no small aspect of effective implementation. It frees up your mind and makes tough calls much easier to face. If you do not get paid on the button on the date, go to your buyer immediately. Don't waste time with accounts payable. If some functionary is balking at your fee or terms, stop work until the buyer resolves the issue. I don't feel any project is under way unless I've been paid.

Gathering Intelligence: Strategy

Ensuring That Data Does Not Equal Intelligence

I can't think of a single project I've undertaken in which I didn't get smarter each day. We are paid to learn in this profession, which is a wondrous thing. But I also can't think of a single project in which I learned everything I needed on the first day, or the second, or the fourteenth.

The more methodical and thorough we are about gathering data, the better our eventual information, knowledge, and intelligence. Preliminary data is just that: a series of often non-valid beliefs, factoids, opinions, mythology, and executive bullying, which pass for information.

A simple example: Many clients have asked me to develop their teamwork at executive or divisional levels, only to abruptly learn that they don't have teams to begin with, but rather committees (which are much more common). I can investigate very quickly to see which construct is in place and can't build a team if the underlying organizational structure is calling for committees.[1] So I have to confront my buyer very early with the news that what he is expecting will require a profoundly more complex approach than what he envisioned.

Since your consulting project's ultimate success will depend largely on the accuracy and validity of your early data gathering, you can't afford to merely accept what client personnel tell you in order to save time or avoid trampling on old turf. The fact is, *there's a reason* why the issues haven't been resolved prior and why an external resource had to be brought in. And that reason *is not* that the internal people have the matter already well in hand, figured out, and scoped.

They don't have a clue, which is why they need you.

CHALLENGING BASIC PREMISES

I call this step the "push back" approach, and it's useful pre-sale but mandatory post-sale. All clients will have basic premises—tenets, beliefs, theorems— which have taken the form of canonical truths. But unlike Jefferson and the Constitution, such "truths" are not self-evident. Don't blindly accept them.

Ultimata: The higher you go in the hierarchy, the more profound the "truths" and the more unchallenged they are, which means that you have to push back hardest at high altitudes. Make sure you have plenty of reserve oxygen for the effort.

Among the "truths" I've encountered in highly regarded Fortune 1000 organizations:

---

1. Just one criterion, as an example: Committee members collaborate only to the degree that they must without sacrificing their own ability to succeed. Rewards are individually oriented, not group based. Team members are forced to share resources, information, and credit because none of them can "win" unless all of them do. You can see why the latter is much rarer than the former in the organizational landscape.

- You can't promote Asians into management ranks because they are too conciliatory to confront people effectively.
- Our customers refuse to learn how to use our hardware, which is why we have such high service costs.
- The salespeople will sell anything at any price without regard to profit or quality, and we have to keep them on a short leash.
- We'd never get anything done if we allowed any employee or any customer to contact our executives freely.
- This product must be a loss leader for us, since we cannot make a margin on it.
- Our competition would severely undercut any efforts we made in that market.
- We cannot get legislative or regulatory approval for this, so we're not going to try.
- The employees would steal us blind if we let them.
- We can't hire from the outside because you have to know this business intimately in order to manage effectively here.
- There is simply no market for this.

I've had clients claim that their employee retention rates were lower than they were by a factor of over 50 percent once I investigated. I've had to parry "facts" that the client was paying a competitive wage when I was able to learn quickly that the competition was 20 percent ahead in every category. And I've had to painfully point out that the interviews I was conducting did not support the belief that the executive vice president was highly regarded and thought to be a great leader.

Ultimata: The problem with accepting bad data is that it will ultimately cast doubt on *all information.* Only by pushing back early and often will you be able to discriminate between reliable sources and unreliable supposition.

Listen carefully to what you're told early on by the buyer, by implementers, and by interested (or disinterested) others. Ask yourself, and then ask

I was meeting with the CEO of a large specialty chemical operation who wanted me to study how to increase sales to compensate for "uncontrolled attrition." The company was losing an astonishing 25 percent of customers each year, resulting in flat growth.

"What is 'uncontrolled attrition'?" I asked.

"It occurs when customers go out of business, have to shut down for long periods, we are overwhelmed by technology we can't match from competitors, and so on," replied the CEO.

"Is 25 percent the industry average?"

"We have no way of knowing."

"How do you know the causes so clearly?"

"We conducted a survey."

"Who conducted a survey?"

"Our field force." Oh, oh.

"Do you really think that your field force would tell you if your clients were actually leaving due to poor service?"

"What are you suggesting?"

What I was suggesting was that I validate the premise with ex-customers, and when I did so I found that eleven of twelve had left due to poor field service. I pointed out that increasing sales might be needed, but reducing attrition was the first order of the day. Every suggestion I made after that was golden.

---

them, "What is the support for that position?" Rely solely on objective, supported fact and observed behavior. Don't allow opinion and bias to hold equal rank. The statement, "He has been late for three meetings in a row by at least thirty minutes each time," is an objective statement that can be tested readily if you haven't actually experienced the behavior yourself. But the statement, "He is constantly late because he's not a team player and he is exhibiting purposeful disrespect for me in front of my staff," is a huge leap.

Managers have a hard enough time being managers. They make lousy pop psychologists.

My Rules of Thumb for Accepting Data

- If it's minor, don't worry about it at all (e.g., the amount of times the copier has been out of action).
- If you've seen it personally, you can accept it, although not necessarily its historical accuracy.
- If you can validate it from two objective sources, you can accept it.
- If you can find it documented from objective sources, you can accept it (e.g., the financial department's breakdown of relocation costs, as reimbursed).
- If it is unsolicited, be careful, and never accept it without the above safeguards; unsolicited feedback is almost always due to a private agenda.
- If patterns emerge from different streams (e.g., focus groups, interviews, surveys, and personal observation) they are usually absolutely safe.
- Finally, always consider the source. The sales department complaining about marketing's poor lead generation, R&D complaining about a lack of funding from finance, and everyone complaining about the sloth of human resources are hardly neutral and balanced complaints in any environment.

Alan's Theorem: Once is an accident, twice is a coincidence, and three times is a pattern.

ENSURING ALTERNATIVE SOURCES OF INFORMATION

Consultants, no less than executives, need their own sources of information within client systems. Otherwise, your inputs will be "filtered," even with the best of intentions, and you'll increasingly build a knowledge base that resembles a house of cards in a brisk wind.

Alternative sources of information are not subversive, secretive, or seductive. They are merely the means to ensure that you are developing an accurate picture and proper responses. Fortunately, there are quite a few simple methods to accomplish this.

Ultimata: Don't talk. Listen. Don't ask "yes or no" questions, but rather those that require substantive feedback. Ask for examples and instances to support the belief. Ask yourself, "If I were going to trial, is this enough evidence?" If you feel that's overly dramatic, remember that you're often influencing people's careers and corporate direction.

Here are some great ways to gain access to unfiltered and unfettered information.

Alan's Ten Methods to Gather Intelligence

1. *Eat in the organization's cafeteria.* Sit at the long tables with employees. Smile and make friends. Just listen to what is being discussed. If people are enraged about the change in the benefit plan every time you listen, the belief from the communications department that "people have accepted it and moved on" is probably bogus.

2. *While working with implementers, listen to their conversations and "prime the pump" with some casual questions.* Mention, for example, during a break in your meeting, "I heard some people saying something about a new benefits plan. What's that all about?"

3. *Ask anyone who volunteers information for examples, frequency, and who else was there.* Never accept anything that's not independently verifiable.

4. *Develop closer relationships with those implementers who demonstrate a track record with you of accuracy and validity.* Disregard the opinions from those who are consistently inaccurate or overtly biased.

5. *Absolutely observe confidentiality (so long as your client's welfare isn't directly threatened) so that people come to trust you.* Trust is hard to earn, but it's virtually impossible to earn back once it's abrogated.

6. *Talk to customers.* They will be highly objective and will usually have their own specific incidents to report.

7. *Use trade and industry periodicals and research.* Find out whether the client organization is really above or below industry averages.

8. *Talk to key suppliers and vendors.* The parts manufacturer will be able to tell you about how easy it is to be paid, and the public relations firm will be able to cite the ease with which they can access key executives.

9. *Keep checking back with the buyer.* He or she has a vested interest in your joint success. Ask if the information you've been developing meshes with his or her beliefs and expectations. Ask if there are other people with whom you should check.

10. *Trust your instincts and history.* At this stage of your career, you've performed in many environments. Ask yourself whether the information basically jibes with reality as you know it. If you're hearing that productivity is low, but people are dashing about in a mad scramble while putting in sixty-hour weeks, you know it's not due to lack of a strong work ethic.

Ultimata: I'm always searching for "incongruities." Companies claiming high morale don't have acres of empty desks while employees are taking two-hour lunches. There shouldn't be harsh cartoons about other departments if there is a "spirit of cross-functional collaboration."

Finally, shop the business yourself. Call the service number; make a complaint; visit a retail outlet; order something small, if possible; ask a difficult question. There is nothing more conclusive than shopping the client's business on several different occasions. The way in which you're treated and the patterns that result will tell you more than any manager would or could. (And, if you want to validate comparisons, shop the competition's business. You'll bring executive meetings to a halt when you explain the positive or negative deviations.)

A note here about confidentiality as you gain access to more and more potential sources of information. My policy, when asked, "Will this be kept confidential?" is the following: I will absolutely maintain confidentiality *except* when I determine that what I'm told has a direct impact on my client's well-being. In other words, if three key officers are about to jump ship, I will not keep

I walked into a client's local restaurant with my wife and surreptitiously timed everything, from the greeting on my arrival, to being seated, to being offered a drink, as well as whether or not the server tried to coax me into a dessert (one of the most profitable items on the menu, along with alcoholic beverages). I tested whether the wait staff could explain dishes, make exceptions to the menu offerings, and suggest a wine.

After three such visits, I was able to tell the regional manager that my informal study tended to support his superiors' claims that his profitability problems were the result of poor local management, not the economy or the local competition. In other words, his bosses were right—his subordinates were covering up.

Sound simple? Remember what I said at the outset about common sense.

---

quiet about it. If people in the warehouse are stealing computers, I will inform the proper manager. If there is sexual harassment going on, I will expose it. It is unethical not to, and the determination of what to withhold and what to expose must be at the sole discretion of the consultant.

By informing the other parties of that condition, you are acting ethically toward them. I will not expose a private grievance or hurt, nor an opinion about a manager, nor a "shortcut" that employees have created to avoid their own bureaucracy. But if there is cheating on expense reports, I will make that public.

Ultimata: You must create your own ethical baseline when you're gathering data. Don't listen to information unless the conditions are clear. And always remember that your client is the buyer. He or she is the one who "brung ya." If the buyer can't trust you to protect his or her best interests, then why should you be trusted at all?

AVOIDING INTIMIDATION—YOURS AND THEIRS

A new client can intimidate a consultant. And a new consultant hovering can intimidate any new client. The trick is to avoid both extremes.

Let's begin with you. Realize that no one can actually intimidate you—you allow others to intimidate you. No matter how much the veteran you may be, we all find ourselves in front of tough managers, multi-million-dollar executives, high-pressure situations, posh offices, and luxury surroundings. (The first night I met a CEO in Sydney, he took me out on his eighty-foot cabin cruiser, complete with crew, canapés, and drinks on the fantail and his current girlfriend, who appeared to be at the very least the reigning Miss Asia Pacific.)

Here are some devices to avoid allowing yourself to be intimidated.

Alan's Ten Tricks to Avoid Being Cowed

1. *Establish a comfortable, first-name relationship.* Don't laugh. I was once in a meeting where subordinates called the president "Mr. President." Ask quickly at the outset how your partner prefers being addressed. A subordinate once called me "Al" for ages, even though I told him I prefer "Alan." I held it against him for ages.[2]

2. *Never pose as an expert.* Position yourself as a partner, advisor, or external colleague. Once you're up on the pedestal, the only travel direction is downward. You're not there to fix the problems that the poor, bumbling internal people couldn't fathom. You're there to provide more help dealing with difficult challenges.

3. *When challenged, don't defend yourself with credentials or explanations of your background.* Simply point out that the buyer was sufficiently convinced that your experiences and competencies were an excellent match for the organization's needs and, if you must, provide examples from other clients. "Here's what we encountered at Citibank when the same issues arose" is an excellent retort.

---

2. Many of these might have been accomplished in the sales process, but not always; furthermore, you'll be meeting people during the project who weren't part of the sales process.

I was introduced to a mid-level manager in his cubicle at Hewlett-Packard, after being told that he was important politically and could ease the way to gain access to various parts of the business. He clearly didn't like an outsider involved and proceeded to ask me about my college degree, content knowledge of network servers, other clients, and just about everything else but blood type.

I responded cordially to the first four or five questions, then said, "Look, I'd love to continue to bore you with my background, but right now time is precious. The general manager (three levels above him) and I both agreed that the project made sense for me, and he suggested that you and I work together, if possible. So can we agree that's possible and move forward? I really don't feel the need to pass some kind of litmus test at this point."

We moved on. He still didn't like me much, but he worked with me. If I had continued to try to jump through his hoops, I simply would have enabled and emboldened his attempts to intimidate me.

Ultimata: It's understandable that some people in the client organization will try to derail your train. But it's unthinkable that you should be out there with a crowbar helping them get leverage. The more you give in, the more they'll expect you to give; the more you stand firm, the more they'll eventually respect you.

---

4. *Try to meet on neutral turf.* See people in conference rooms, in the cafeteria, in the dining room, even offsite. Try not to always be taking a seat across the desk from someone whose chair seems to be several inches taller than yours.

5. *Push back firmly and whenever the situation calls for it.* Once you weakly agree to something that is not appropriate (or plain wrong), all the remaining requests and direction, no matter how friendly and congenial, will be built on this fundamentally ineffective direction. Trying to reverse it later means either that you were too stupid to realize the suggestion was so poor or too

cowardly to mention it at the time. Don't allow volume or numbers to carry a poor suggestion through the defenses.

6. *Never accept a political role or take sides.* As projects unfold, you'll often discover a "revenge" agenda or prejudicial objectives that weren't apparent at the outset. Eschew all attempts to involve you in vendettas. Find cause, not blame. I've lost several accounts in which I was too eager to side with a very senior person who seemed to have all the "juice," only to find out the hard way that someone else was a more powerful or more clever political operative. I became the expended cannon fodder.

7. *Be proactive.* Don't place yourself in the position where you're meeting people merely to answer questions or to bring them up-to-date. Ask provocative questions. Challenge their thinking. Obtain their opinions on a controversial issue. Force people to provide value to you and to the project.

8. *Do your homework.* Become at least conversant in the client's business and the client's customers. If you hear acronyms and technical jargon repeatedly, find out what it means. Understand the company history and culture. (I actually know a consultant who drove up to a Ford plant in a new Toyota, oblivious to the fact that this was considered a personal insult. Rent a Ford, if you must.)

9. *Face setbacks honestly.* Don't allow people to start invoking doom the first moment the project doesn't proceed as planned. Educate people from the start that no project proceeds unhindered and unwaveringly from inception to conclusion, and then address the problems openly and honestly. (And don't *blame* anyone, not even yourself. Simply find the *cause* and remove it.)

10. *Understand that tomorrow's another day.* If you had a bad day or a bad encounter, then plan how to "undo" it or correct it tomorrow. Don't accept a temporary setback as a terminal defeat, and don't allow your client colleagues to see it that way either. Use tomorrow to improve, not to sulk.

Ultimata: Intimidation is a response to threat. If you reduce the threat—yours or theirs—you eliminate the need to intimidate. Some people, however, are *always* threatened. That's their problem, not yours.

Now let's take a look at the other side of the coin. Even though others allow themselves to be intimidated, you still have the option of reducing the likelihood by controlling your own behavior and demeanor.

There is a certain ego need attached to some levels of immaturity which causes people to try to elevate themselves by demeaning others. That's bad behavior and bad business. Accept the fact that we're all equals, undamaged, who would like to share in win/win situations, and you're off to a great start in establishing a comfortable relationship.

Alan's Ten Tricks to Avoid Cowing Others

1. *Don't start by talking.* Start by listening. You need to learn about your new colleagues and their expectations, fears, and experiences. You can't do that by talking. Begin every new conversation with provocative questions and practice active listening.

2. *Don't start with your process, methodology, or approach.* Wait to learn something about the environment, culture, and the implementers themselves. This will tell you the best way to introduce your approach and will also tell you how you may have to modify it to make it optimally successful and accepted.

3. *Stop dropping the buyer's name.* People will think you're "the boss's man" or a spy in their midst. Moreover, they will decide, prudently, not to share anything with you that might find its way back to people who can hurt them or retaliate against them.

4. *Join them in the cafeteria.* Avoid the executive dining room. Hang out casually where they do. Having a beer with the assembly line people is a lot more important (and usually more fun) than having a martini with the plant manager.

5. *Contribute to company causes.* There is often a collection in operation for the disadvantaged, a charity which the company supports, or some special need. Make your donation. You can ask how best to do it to ensure that others know you're participating.

6. *Observe social mores.* If the person who takes the last cup of coffee has to make a new pot, then that would be you at times. Clean up after yourself. Don't use a fax, copier, or company phone without the permission of people in the area. Demonstrate a respect for the workplace and the work habits. If an office is important for your project, make sure it's mod-

est and reasonable, and not a corner executive "palace." Keep the door open.

7. *Dress like everyone else.* You don't want to be an "imported suit," nor do you want to be someone who's more casual than the normal rules would allow. Don't stand out in a crowd, at least sartorially.

8. *Maintain confidences.* With the admonition discussed earlier that "secrets" which materially impact the buyer can't be honored, do respect all those that don't impact the buyer. Do not feed the grapevine or engage in gossip.

9. *Don't take sides.* Even in minor skirmishes where you feel one side is clearly sinning and the other is on the side of the angels, don't lobby one way or the other unless your project is directly threatened by the impasse or unfairness. Attempting to be political in an environment whose politics long pre-date your arrival is simply suicidal. If you win, you'll intimidate the losers; if you lose, you'll appear to be an amateur.

10. *Show humility.* Share credit. Be heard and seen telling the buyer openly that it was the implementers who gained the victory, that you just provided some advice. It's difficult to intimidate people whom you're hailing for their tremendous achievement.

Ultimata: Never, ever give an order to any client personnel. Ask every assistant, secretary, and support person for permission, and maintain unfailing courtesy toward all. Consulting projects rapidly fail when consultants set themselves up with authority and no responsibility. In fact, you have responsibility but no real authority.

WALKING THE CONFIDENTIALITY TIGHTROPE

Before we begin examining specific interventions, it's worthwhile to discuss the specifics of confidentiality and observing ethical commitments of silence.

Whatever the buyer tells you is confidential *must remain so.* If you feel that confidentiality is inappropriate—let's say that the buyer has informed you the entire division will be sold and there will be massive layoffs at a time you're engaged in trying to build long-term loyalty and prevent defections—then you have the option of attempting to talk your buyer out of the confidential demand. If that doesn't work, you then have the option of ceasing work and refunding a pro-rata share of the fee.

But what you can't do is simply ignore the buyer's request for confidence. Your choices are

- Accept the constraint
- Try to change the buyer's mind
- Remove yourself from the project

You have choices. You don't have such choices with employee requests for secrecy. Your position must be that you cannot withhold information from the buyer which affects the buyer's (and the client's) well-being. You will be sole judge of that affect.

I believe the criteria which justify not upholding a confidence (which is not the same as betraying one, since you're making this clear prior to being told anything) include

- Stealing and corruption
- Key people planning to leave
- Key accounts planning to defect
- Faulty intelligence that will undermine the company's strategy
- Potential for damaging lawsuits (e.g., violation of the Americans with Disabilities Act, bias in the hiring process, and so on)
- Harm being done to employees (sexual harassment, discrimination)
- Harm being done to customers (quality problems, defects, sabotage)

Ultimata: You are not an independent observer, but a hired counselor whose loyalty must be to the buyer and the organization represented by that buyer. If you abrogate that trust by withholding key information from your client, you have by definition taken the other side on that issue. That is tantamount to treason.

The ideal statement is quite simple when you're confronted with a request for confidentiality:

I cannot withhold something from my buyer and this client which may have serious impact, such as legal, safety, competitive, and similar issues. I will have to be the sole judge of that impact. So if you're comfortable with the fact that I may choose not to uphold the confidentiality, you may tell me. But you cannot rely on your information remaining a secret. If this is something that you believe impacts the company strongly, I would encourage you to tell Janet Hopkins personally.

Note that you can't even guarantee that the name will be withheld, because credibility and rapid response will demand that the person who came forward be contacted in many instances. You are a consultant hired by the organization through the buyer, not an independent journalist reporting objective events and seeking to protect sources.

Figure 2.1 shows the relationship of the three elements required for proper ethical conduct. As the consultant, you must be in a "will act" position at all times: aware of the environment, possessing the values to know right from wrong, and competent in the skills required to take the proper actions.

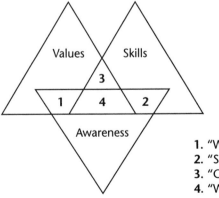

1. "Would act" but can't, because of lack of skills
2. "Should act" but won't, because of lack of values
3. "Could act" but doesn't, because of lack of awareness
4. "Will act" because all elements are present

Figure 2.1. Requisites for Proper Ethical Conduct

At Astra Pharmaceuticals in the mid-90s, there was widespread sexual harassment emanating from the highest levels in the U.S. organization. The CEO was ultimately forced to resign as legal discovery uncovered the extent and duration of the illegal practices. Wholesale changes had to be made within the U.S. corporate structure.

How could this have occurred for so long, despite widespread knowledge, a human resources and legal function, and outside consultants regularly employed for a variety of projects? Because no one chose to do anything about it. And because the top officer locally was apparently a part of it.

Your commitment is to your buyer. But if your buyer is engaging in unethical practices, then your commitment is to your client as a whole. There is always someone to whom to appeal: a higher level officer, a parent company, a general counsel, a human resources vice president, a conscientious subordinate.

The bottom line must always be, in any project, to do the right thing.

FINAL THOUGHT

Don't "look the other way" too often, or you'll find that you are no longer able to look straight ahead. Confront difficulties, ambiguities, and questionable conduct early. Otherwise, they will either escalate and be much harder to reverse, or they will have enveloped you, making you a silent partner to the deeds.

Gathering Intelligence: Tactics

Ensuring That Information Does Not Equal Intelligence

From this point forward, now that we have discussed the proper methods to establish the groundwork for your intervention, we'll focus on the interventions themselves. A few words are in order to soothe the soon-to-be apoplectic.

First, it's impossible to cover every single consulting methodology, from conflict resolution and team building to expert witnesses and facilitation. This book is about *process* not about *content*, and my intent is that the principles and approaches you find here can be applied to your circumstances, no matter how mainstream and generic or esoteric and abstruse they may be.

Second, please don't blow the fuses because you don't do it the way I do it (or vice versa). This series is for experienced and successful consultants, so the probability of your doing something different from me is relatively high. I'm not suggesting that my way is better, but I have to begin with something, and I know my way better than your way.

Which leads me to third: I have chosen a variety of specific techniques I have found to be among the most needed, requested, practiced, pragmatic, and sometimes abused. There is a need not to allow a conceptual, ideological discussion to overwhelm the practical need to demonstrate how methodologies should be implemented.

So view the remainder of this book as a guide to implementing consulting methodologies, with a couple of dozen selected for the purposes of illustration and example. This is not a compendium or encyclopedia of the full gamut of consulting alternatives. For that, you'd have to go to . . . well, actually, I have no idea where you'd go because I doubt that it exists. Let's try to make do with my selections for now.

HOW TO FOCUS A FOCUS GROUP

Focus groups are small selections of people (I've seen them done well from six to twenty-five participants) assembled for the purpose of gathering information about their experiences, preferences, opinions, reactions, and so on. They may be employees, customers, former customers, prospective customers, vendors, the public at large, or any other sample which makes sense for the purposes of the information desired.

The key is to begin with *the information that is desired.* You can't assemble the alternative (the group's demographic) until you understand what it is you're trying to learn. Egregiously, non-customers can't give you a customer experience, but more subtly, a relatively new employee can't help you much with changes in the culture or work environment.

Ultimata: Make people comfortable at focus groups. Invest in coffee and snacks. Encourage some icebreaking. The more at ease the individuals, the more they will tend to volunteer opinions. Don't forget that you're already an outsider who may seem threatening even before you ask a question.

THE BALANCE SHEET ON FOCUS GROUPS

The great advantages of focus groups are

- They are self-sanctioning, wherein one or two participants, no matter how vociferous, may be countered by the majority pointing out that they have not based opinions on objective fact.
- You can ask follow-up questions.
- You can ask for specific examples and behaviors to validate expressed views.
- They can be assembled by demographic: gender, age, work assignment, education, and so on, or be completely drawn at random.
- They are anonymous[1] and can provide "real time" feedback as often as you require it.
- In certain circumstances, they can be observed through one-way glass or through recordings.

The disadvantages of focus groups include

- Some people will fear being quoted by a colleague in the room and will keep quiet, despite assurances of anonymity.
- They can be dominated by a few people with personal agendas and loud voices.
- They can be affected by very recent events which may or may not have anything to do with the topic at hand. For example, a change in the compensation system will almost always create negativity in focus groups, even though the purported subject matter is the cafeteria food.

I believe that the following are the mandatory and remaining steps for running a successful focus group.

Ten Steps to a Successful Focus Group
1. *Gather a random selection of people from the desired demographic.* This should be done with a random number sequence (e.g., every fourth name) or by

---

1. Although that depends on the character of the participants much more than on the commitment of the facilitator.

random selection by computer. Do not allow supervisors or managers to select participants.

Ultimata: Run a focus group the way the trains should be run: on time, on the track, and to the right station. You are neither the engineer nor the conductor. You're the track maintenance guy.

2. *Send a letter from the senior sponsor of the program to every participant chosen.* Issue a polite invitation which includes the fact that attendance is mandatory (otherwise you will suffer self-selection and deselection), the logistics, and the expectations. A sample letter is shown in Exhibit 3.1.
3. *Invite to any one session about three more people than you need.* This is to account for the inevitable no-shows. In the worst case, accommodate three extra people. If you want fifteen participants, invite eighteen and have eighteen chairs and sets of refreshments available.
4. *Start on time.* Begin by establishing the "rules of engagement," for example:

- Everyone is welcome to contribute whenever they like
- No one will be quoted, and you expect everyone present to observe their colleagues' anonymity (no name tents, rosters, or sign-in sheets)
- Everyone should be heard, and there should be no personal attacks or defensiveness
- You will be taking notes for the purpose of accuracy, which you'll be happy to review at the conclusion
- The feedback will be used in conjunction with other groups for (whatever the project objectives are)
- This will take no longer than ninety minutes (or whatever is allotted) and might end early if the energy runs out
- Are there any questions?[2]

---

2. If you're running a "fishbowl" focus group in which participants are observed or heard, you should make this clear, unless other provisions have been made.

Dear Samantha,

I'm pleased to invite you to the focus group being held on September 20th, from 1:00 to 2:30 p.m. in Conference Room C, fourth floor of the headquarters building. It will be facilitated by Jane Ryan, an external consultant working with us on this project.

The focus group, which is one of a dozen being held around the company, is intended to gather employee ideas about how to more rapidly respond to customer inquiries, since the average wait at the moment is nearly ten minutes, which we consider much too long. Your name was chosen at random, but your opinion and ideas are highly important, so your participation is mandatory. If, for any reason, you cannot meet on this date and time, please notify my assistant, Carole Reid, at extension 104 immediately.

Your participation will be confidential and will be cleared with your direct manager. Please plan to be at the meeting room no later than ten minutes prior to the start time. You'll find refreshments available there beginning thirty minutes before the start time.

Thanks for taking the time to help us with this important project. Feel free to call me directly should you have any questions.

Sincerely,

Jack Spenser
Senior Vice President

Exhibit 3.1.   Sample Focus Group Invitation

5. *Begin by asking a provocative question to "prime the pump."* In other words, if the compensation system is the subject, you might ask, "How would you characterize the current compensation system?" or "How do you think the compensation system compares with those of your chief competitors?"

> *Ultimata:* Encourage participation. Challenge unsupported claims. Provoke people a bit. You should be willing to cause some constructive dissension if you have reason to believe you're not hearing substantive comments or facts.

6. *Continue to ask a few provocative questions and/or follow-up questions as the participants warm up.* Work with each point until you feel it is exhausted.
7. *Cut off soliloquies and constant interruptions from the same person.* Simply say, "I appreciate your views, but my charge is to hear from as many different people as possible" or "If you don't mind, I'd like to get the others' views on that subject."
8. *Periodically summarize points.* This will both ensure your accuracy and help the group to continue to think through the issues.
9. *Don't be bashful about asking people who have remained quiet to contribute from time to time.* They always have the option not to do so, but you should make sure, while you're with them, that you encourage as many people to contribute as possible.
10. *Never take sides.* But do become the devil's advocate at times to challenge assumptions that everyone seems to believe but which no one can really back up with evidence.

My suggestion is to always use a laptop to record your notes, since you can more easily assemble them and edit for clarity. Handwritten notes are also fine, but require twice the work.

> *Ultimata:* All sampling methods will have intrinsic weaknesses and vulnerabilities. However, when you use several in concert, you can maximize the strengths while offsetting the individual drawbacks. I always prefer to see *evidence* and observe *behavior* to support what people claim.

I had decided to run focus groups as part of Merck's baseline study of its approaches to diversity in the company. The groups were deliberately varied: some all female, some all male, some mixed; some were all minority, some all white, some mixed; some were professional level, while others were administrative. All company major sites were included.

The results were nothing less than spectacular. All-white groups bemoaned the "advantages" bestowed upon minorities and felt that women, particularly, could claim any position they liked. Women felt that the glass ceiling was alive and well, and senior positions were only available in "women-acceptable" areas, such as human resources and legal.

African-Americans, in particular, cited harsh grievances with specific facts and behaviors that were simply invisible to their white colleagues. The report (augmented by interviews, surveys, and observations) jolted senior management, but the company responded well and has consistently been hailed as one of America's "most admired companies" by the annual *Fortune* magazine polls (and the company had actually finished in first place over a period of several consecutive years).

Note: Some groups advertise seminars and workshops to "certify" people in facilitation skills (or coaching skills, or, presumably, breathing skills). I've found that veteran consultants often enroll, especially when they are moving to a new methodology. My question is always this: "Who certifies the certifiers? Who created them as the experts??"

You need careful instruction to defuse bombs. You would require strict discipline to perform open heart surgery. You may well need coaching to sew a hem. But believe me, if you've been a successful consultant you have the requisite smarts and talents to conduct a focus group without anyone granting you a diploma.

If you absolutely require certification for your self-esteem, send me $100 and I'll send you a lovely document suitable for framing.

HOW TO CONDUCT AN INTERVIEW

I'm speaking here of interviews as part of an intervention strategy, with the aim of soliciting information about specific issues. These are pre-arranged and, to some extent, choreographed.

The advantages of interviews are that they are personal and intimate, and support anonymity. Successive interviewees cannot—without collusion—deliberately support or debunk what preceded them. The disadvantages are that (1) people can be intimidated by the one-on-one intimacy, (2) there is no sanctioning of what they say so they can claim almost anything, and (3) there is no larger group to which to appeal to further explore an issue.

The successful interviewing process should include

- An invitation letter, similar to the focus group letter
- A private interview area, where participants can meet with you in private and not be seen arriving or departing[3]
- Enough time between interviews so that participants don't see each other arriving and departing (You can also accomplish this by alternating between two interview offices on two different floors)
- A more formalized (than the focus group) list of questions so that the interviewer can guarantee comparisons, contrasts, and patterns will emerge (You want to be sure to ask everyone the same questions, even if follow-up questions go in different directions)
- What I call a "cumulative memory," so that issues that arise in early interviews that are a surprise to you are pursued in later ones (In focus groups that is less necessary, since the entire group can be asked about new issues; in interviews, it's essential to validate or invalidate with ongoing interviewees)
- Note taking and summarizing for the participants, as in the focus group process

I favor interviews that are set up for forty-five minutes but which may take much less time. Contrary to most "conventional wisdom," I've found that after

---

3. For all such interventions, I strongly advocate that the client be the one accountable for the scheduling, room, and supporting logistics.

about twenty minutes the conversation tends to become redundant or irrelevant. It helps to be highly directive in interviews. Some examples:

- "I think we're getting off course, so let me rephrase the question to try to refocus us."
- "I'm not sure I heard the answer to my question. May I ask you again?"
- "Actually, an example or specific incident of what you're describing would be most helpful here."

Finally, use the therapists' great device of allowing silences to linger. An interviewee who is reluctant to offer much will often wade into a silence because it is too uncomfortable not to do so. Provide encouragement for the responses: "Ah, that's a great point. Let me make sure I get it down accurately."

Ultimata: People love to hear the sound of their own voices. Try repeating simply the last word they say ("contracts?") and allow them to elaborate. Ninety-nine times out of one hundred, they will provide more details just with that lone prompt.

HOW TO CREATE AND IMPLEMENT SURVEYS

Surveys are wonderful instruments because they enable you to reach a wide variety of people. While focus groups and interviews must be restricted to a limited sample of the population, surveys can be provided for an entire workforce, customer base, vendor list, and so on.

The drawback of surveys is that they are famous for self-selection. That is, those with a particular agenda, grievance, or bias are most likely to respond and most likely to respond vociferously. Those who are more or less content—or apathetic—will tend not to respond at all. How do you tell whether the often silent majority are happy or hapless? You can't. (Which is why a combination of focus groups, interviews, and surveys really serves the client best. Consistent patterns which emerge from all three devices tend to be highly reliable.)

Here are the rules for an effective survey.

1. Begin with an Agreement on What You Want to Know. You and the client must agree on what the information is to be used for. This is why I don't like off-the-shelf instruments. (That, and the fact that you're providing much higher value if you custom-design a survey for a client. Anyone can simply buy a pre-packaged device.) Too many surveys contain irrelevant questions and tangential inquiries. (As long as we're sending this survey on commuting to them, can we also ask them about their breakfast preferences?) Hone this down to the narrowest comfortable inquiry. The highest quality survey responses are from crisp, precise, and brief instruments.

Ultimata: The key to a survey isn't how much you *ask* but rather how much you *learn.* You're always better off learning a great deal in a few areas than a little bit in a great number of areas. Keep surveys as brief as possible.

---

2. Select the Demographic. Are you sending this to everyone, to a certain age group, to a certain level of experience, or to exactly whom? If it's to go to a wide variety or random selection of people but demographic information is important in evaluating the responses, make sure that you include the appropriate categories within the instrument (e.g., have you worked here for fewer than five years, five to ten years, or more than ten years, and so on).

3. Design the Instrument. Design the instrument based on the information sought. Whether electronic or hard copy,[4] most surveys contain some variation of the following:

- Include a brief set of instructions at the beginning. There is also usually a cover letter or paragraph on the purpose. A sample question and proper

---

4. Both are effective. Hard copy can take longer to collate and evaluate; electronic means are subject to scrambling, loss, and even hacking. I've not seen data that indicates either has a higher rate of return than the other, all factors being equal.

I was asked to conduct a survey at Astra Pharmaceuticals. The new human resources vice president wanted to gather some information in the aftermath of a dramatic management shakeup which would help her set policies and respond to employee needs.

In the midst of designing it, she asked if we could make it a part of the annual employee survey that was about to be administered anyway, a massive document on company morale, service, benefits, needs, commuting, food subsidies, and so on. In an attempt to be helpful and flexible, I agreed.

Then she asked if I could also merge another set of completely unrelated questions on diversity for another consulting firm she had hired for that purpose. This time reluctantly, but no less foolishly, I agreed.

The result was a fiasco. The participant return was slightly better than past averages (probably because of the need to comment after the management upheaval), but the data was so diffused, confusing, and contradictory that there wasn't much value. In fact, the vice president's specific instruction to me was not to ask about race or ethnicity in the demographic section, yet the diversity firm specifically needed that "cut" of data to make sense of other responses.

We quickly parted ways. I deserved it. My zeal to please a new client overshadowed my professional duty to do it right. I don't have to learn that lesson again. The buyer is better served when you tell her she's wrong.

---

response are helpful. If a particular type of pen or pencil is required, note that. Also provide a return address in case the return mailer is lost. Finally, the deadline for responding should be clear.

- Questions may be multiple choice (agree strongly, agree somewhat, disagree somewhat, disagree strongly), binary (agree/disagree, yes/no, would/would not), numeric (rated on a 1 to 10 or other scale), or narrative (describe in a few sentences how you would improve customer service). My preference is to always include a few narrative questions, which enable the respondent to provide more qualitative feedback.

Ultimata: Avoid ambiguity in surveys. If you use a 1 to 5 scale, for example, explain what each number represents, not just the extremes. There is nothing more frustrating than someone who has taken the time to respond but has not completed the instrument correctly.

- Ask for demographic information, which may include age, tenure, education, salary level, gender, and so on. Be careful with small samples so as not to inadvertently reveal the respondent through the combination of demographic responses (e.g., there is only one female manager in R&D working here more than ten years).

Rule of Thumb: Keep the survey as brief as possible while still eliciting the information you require. Put yourself in the respondent's shoes. Completing a survey is not fun, and you'll tend to get lower quality responses toward the end of long surveys. I advocate putting your most important questions toward the front of the survey. Place the least important and the demographic data (which is simple to complete) at the end.

4. Test the Instrument. This is a crucial step often overlooked, even by veteran testing firms. Take a small sample of the intended population and have them complete the survey. Then do two things:

- Evaluate whether the quality and type of feedback are what you had intended to elicit (not the trends, but the ability to establish trends).
- Ask the respondents what difficulties they had (almost like running a focus group about the survey) so that you can smooth these out in the final version. What is often crisply clear to the designer becomes totally opaque to the respondent.

5. Prepare the Audience. Have the key sponsor send an introductory memo, letter, or email to the intended recipients. The letter should explain the purpose and importance of the survey and why they were selected (even if randomly or if everyone is to be asked). Ensure confidentiality and anonymity of individual responses. Offer to share the entire feedback when available. Confirm the deadline. Provide a phone number for questions. Survey response improves when people are prepared in advance for their involvement.

6. Administer and Evaluate. The administration for a survey can be divided. The client can distribute it through normal company channels to save time and money and to ensure saturation. But the returns must go to you. Responses plummet when the participants suspect that company personnel may be reading their feedback, no matter how anonymous the form. (There is virtually always suspicion of hidden "coding" to identify respondents, no less virulent a belief than held by those who think they have been abducted by UFOs.)

Adhere to your deadlines. If you're using electronic correlations, ensure that the program is working correctly by comparing hand-scored samples at random to the overall trends. If you've used narrative responses, record them separately for your client, correlated with other data if appropriate (e.g., males made these comments, while females made quite different observations).

Ultimata: As a consultant and not merely an instrument provider, you can make an evaluation as to whether the survey results jibe with what you see in the environment. If there is a strong deviation from what's written (morale is high) and what you see (people sending out résumés on their computers), then you need to do further assessment work.

Make an assessment as to whether you have valid samples to make conclusions. If you're not using other data-gathering devices with the survey, then ensure that your response rate is sufficient. The best surveys I've seen, sent to general populations, regularly achieve a 50 percent to 65 percent return. Our own record was 85 percent with a major bank. If you obtain a return of less than 30 percent, the data is very suspect in that the self-selection process will have an overwhelming influence on the responses. As many as half or more of the respondents may not be neutral or objective in their reactions.

7. Share the Results.   Aside from your obligations to management in the context of the project, provide participants with at least a summary of the responses. This will provide incentive to participate in the future and will also fulfill a commitment to be open with the feedback. If management does not want results released in writing, then hold several voluntary meetings at which you provide a summary of the findings. (If the summary comes from management, it will be suspect. Ironically, the consultant will have much more credibility.)

Surveys are highly effective instruments and, in all candor, there are firms which specialize in them and provide "state-of-the-art" alternatives. However, any intelligent consultant can employ them and design them and, when using them in conjunction with focus groups and interviews, can generate highly valid and timely information for the client.

STAFFING A "HOT LINE"

I'm not sure where this fits, so I'll mention it here. A "hot line" is usually a telephone number (although it could be email or fax) which allows an employee or customer to voice an opinion, recommendation, or complaint.

We set up a series of hot lines for Calgon when the company was being sold by Merck to English China Clays (ECC). Employees were encouraged to relay their concerns, fears, questions, and any other matters on an anonymous basis. My staff on the phones took down the inquiries, eliminated duplication, and placed them in categories (compensation, relocation, retirement, and so forth). I then forwarded them to the president, who responded to the inquiries by category in a mass memo every Friday.

Ultimata: The purpose of a hot line is to allow people to express the fears, concerns, suggestions, and priorities on their minds at the moment. Don't lead them in any particular direction. However, do ask for examples and specifics so that the responses address precise areas of concern. A retirement package, for example, has a different impact for a new employee than it does for someone entirely vested in the existing package. Which person is making the comment about retirement fears?

I was presenting the results of a particularly contentious survey to the home office employees of AgVet, the former animal health division of Merck. The presentation was being videotaped for remote sites as well.

The questions were hot and heavy, and I could feel the management team sweating behind me. When we had handled the last one, I expected the general manager to rip my head off for suggesting such an open forum to disseminate results.

I was shocked when he asked if I'd be willing to take the debriefing on the road to other sites in person. When he saw my amazement, he laughed: "I'd rather have those comments expressed out loud so that everyone is assured we've heard them than have them muttering that we'd never listen and no one cares. They know we've heard them, and they can see that we care. This was the most useful part of the entire survey!"

As his memos were circulated, the phone inquiries briefly intensified with follow-up questions, then dropped off precipitously, just as we had planned. After the initial surge, people felt more comfortable, more trusting, and more confident about how they would be cared for. After that, everyone got back to work and productivity resumed at normal levels.

Hot lines simply require a battery of phones on toll-free numbers staffed during business hours (although business hours coast-to-coast). You can pay people by the hour to staff them and create templates to be filled out during each call to aid in the collation. My experience has been that women with school-age children are ideal for the job, highly talented but not otherwise occupied during school hours and eager for interesting work. College students are also excellent resources.

Hot lines aren't as directed as are surveys, focus groups, and interviews, but they fit under the heading of information gathering. And they are easy to implement, forming a wonderful additional tool for any consultant involved in a project requiring such outlets.

HOW TO OBSERVE (AND SEE WHAT OTHERS DON'T)

I've mentioned on several occasions the need to make first-hand observations to validate other findings, and, of course, we're often called on to observe an operation or certain behaviors to report back as an impartial observer.

Observation ought to be conducted at different times. And you need to avoid the "Hawthorne Effect"[5] by being casual about it, not by standing around with a clipboard and stopwatch in your hands!

Ultimata: What you observe casually—while engaged in other activities, meetings, and so on—is much more valuable than what you "officially" observe while trying to do nothing else but. When people know you're watching, their behavior will be altered. When they believe they're unobserved, they'll act most naturally.

Among the general behaviors to observe:

- How many times do phones ring before being answered?
- Are desks largely filled with people at work, or are they abandoned?
- Are managers' doors open or closed most of the day?
- Do people take longer than usual lunches and breaks?
- Are there customers waiting in long lines or unapproached?
- Are there "wall-to-wall" meetings in progress every day?
- Is there laughter and good will in the environment, or do people have murmured conversations which cease when someone walks by?
- What is the level of courtesy of people speaking on the phones?
- Do people tend to sit by rank or in cliques in the cafeteria?
- Do you see and/or hear racial or sexual epithets or innuendo?

---

5. The famous study that demonstrated that employee behavior is influenced simply by being observed. When lights were turned up, productivity increased. But when lights were turned down, productivity also increased.

I found a "pin-up" calendar in a supervisor's office in a warehouse during my unscheduled travels to observe behavior in my client's operations. I hadn't seen a nude picture of a woman in a company setting for at least twenty years.

When told that it was against both company policy and the law, the supervisor and his manager told me curtly that it was a warehouse and they weren't expecting any women to be working there any time soon.

I told my client that he was facing a possible lawsuit on the basis of a hostile environment and that his human resource people were probably asleep at the switch if this rather egregious violation could be in evidence for so long.

My client was deeply indebted, and the power of merely observing the workplace as an objective outsider was underscored for me still again.

Don't feel limited in your observations to the particular project at hand. First, you never know what may be relevant or irrelevant. Second, you may be doing your client a favor by reporting on unrelated matters.

Be sure, however, that your observations aren't random or single events. Look for patterns and repetition. One incident of sexual harassment is sufficient for reporting, but one incident of a phone unanswered probably is not.

FINAL THOUGHT

No amount of data is infallible. What you see is always more valid than what's merely reported. Try to engage in the widest samplings with the most diverse mechanisms possible in any particular client environment. Accurate reporting will make you golden. Inaccurate reporting will make you yesterday's consultant.

CHAPTER 4

Coaching Key People

Coaches Offer Candid Advice, Not Cockeyed Certifications

A few years ago everyone was a consultant. Today, everyone is a coach. What's the difference? Beats me.

As usual, I don't have very strong opinions on this matter, except as follows:

- Coaching is a type of business consulting that is focused on individuals rather than on systems, groups, processes, procedures, structure, and so on.
- The components of coaching are quite simple, although the results can be quite dramatic.
- You do not need a degree in psychology to coach people in areas such as business skills, communication, interpersonal relations, presentations, and so forth. None of us, even if we do have a Ph.D. in psychology, should be offering a therapeutic intervention in the guise of business coaching.
- You most certainly don't need a "certification" or "license" from any body or organization to allow you to coach. My

question is always this: Who certifies the certifiers? I believe there are more people offering advice on coaching than there are good coaches.

- Not everyone—no matter how efficacious a consultant—is cut out to be a coach, since the skill requirements are very discrete, just as not all consultants are meant to be expert witnesses, strategy facilitators, or negotiators.

Now that I've said all that, the majority of people reading this chapter have probably coached managers or executives, formally or informally, periodically throughout their careers. My point in this chapter is to provoke you to think about (1) whether you've been doing it as effectively as possible, and, consequently, (2) whether you've really been conveying and capitalizing on the true value you're providing.

OBSERVATIONAL COACHING

The best coaching is the result of hard evidence: actual behavior, speech, actions, and other clearly observable phenomena. The reason I believe that 360° feedback[1] devices are never sufficient in and of themselves is that they rely on hearsay, even when the respondent is citing instances and examples of behavior. In other words, you still haven't seen it yourself.

Ultimata: Coaching is like "tough love." If you're not going to be absolutely candid right from the outset, then find another line of work, because you're not going to make a difference. Coaching involves pain.

Observing your client involves seeing him or her in a variety of settings and situations. "Shadowing," therefore, is an effective mechanism whereby you

---

1. The practice of interviewing subordinates, peers, superiors, and sometimes others (such as customers and vendors) to acquire patterns of behavior for the person being coached to appreciate and modify, as necessary.

spend a prolonged period—anywhere from a half-day to several days at a time—elbow-to-elbow with the client. This includes meetings, phone calls, interviews, customer interactions, employee disciplinary meetings, corporate presentations, and so on. One of the key reasons for this is that clients often dismiss the important and over-dramatize the unimportant in their own assessments.

I've found clients arriving for work at 6 a.m. who are clearly making poorer decisions at 6 p.m. due to fatigue and impatience, yet they never consider their long hours a cause of any problems. I've also found clients who insist that we work on delegation skills, when the real problem is that everyone is petrified to make decisions in an authoritarian culture, *no matter how well the client delegates!* These details and instances of "cognitive dissonance" are key to the change process and are dramatic contributors of value to the engagement.

Most clients will listen to the coach in terms of how the relationship should proceed (see "rules of engagement" below). Therefore, you should strive for the most open and intense view of the client's business life.[2] Arrive when the client arrives, and spend the entire day, with the exception of bathroom breaks and highly confidential meetings but including meals and employee interactions. Your presence in meetings should be explained candidly: "Alan is working with me on personal coaching issues, and part of his assignment is to observe my day. He has signed all necessary non-disclosure documents, and you can speak openly. In fact, just pretend he's not here." Along those lines, you should always try to fade into the background:

- Don't sit at the meeting table, but along the wall.
- Don't pull up a chair to the tête-à-tête, but sit elsewhere, within earshot.
- If you're taking notes, use a pen and small pad, not a laptop or digital device.
- Never, ever offer a comment or intervene, no matter what's happening, short of physical violence.
- Don't offer ongoing feedback to your client, even if asked. Wait for the designated feedback meetings.

---

2. Let me anticipate an issue here: The more intimate the business view, the more you will learn about the client's personal life, from family relationships and hobbies to illnesses and obligations.

- Do not engage in non-verbal behavior or exchange communication with anyone else in the room.

My experience is that if you do this over a prolonged period—say one or two full days at a time—the client will not be able to maintain a façade to show you a picture that isn't accurate under normal (non-observed) circumstances. That's the beauty of shadowing for longer stretches. If you do it for only half a day at certain intervals, your client if much more able to advertently or inadvertently present a set of behaviors that is due to your presence only.

Ultimata: Make sure you observe your client at the beginning of the day, mid-day, and at the end of the day. Energy levels vary and are a key determinant of behavior. Also, Monday mornings and Friday afternoons can be quite revealing when compared to mid-week.

Here are some typical things to watch for and note when observing your clients.

Observational Checklist
- Does the environment influence behavior? Does your client act differently in his or her office, in other peoples' offices, at meals, offsite, and so on?
- Does the other performer influence behavior? Is he or she markedly different with subordinates, peers, superiors, customers, people from other departments, and so forth?
- Does your client's apparent energy level influence behavior?
- Does stress influence behavior? Does he or she become more thoughtful or more imprudent when deadlines approach or a crisis occurs?
- Do personal concerns influence behavior? What happens when he or she is concerned about a raise, an assignment, or a worrisome call from home?
- Does ego influence behavior? Does your client take resistance personally? Is he constantly seeing "enemies" at the gates? Does she tend to feel "disrespected" over minor slights or imagined intentions?

As I observed a divisional president for prolonged periods, his habit of finishing other peoples' sentences and providing "even better" ways to do their work was painfully and consistently apparent. He was ferociously bright, knew the business better than anyone else, and could keep voluminous amounts of information in his head.

He continually reported that he thought meetings had gone well, but was disappointed with the relative lack of contribution from his subordinates. As he was unwilling to believe that he was, in fact, intimidating them daily with his "helpful suggestions," I finally recorded a session. When we listened to the playback he was aghast at his own behavior.

"Why didn't anyone point this out to me?" he asked somewhat naively.

"If you were in that room as a participant," I asked, "at what point would you have broken in to tell the boss that he was being overbearing, assertive, and threatening?"

We made two changes immediately thereafter: We reduced the number of meetings he attended, and we modified his behavior in the meetings he did attend. It was tough for him to do this, but the productivity of his people rose dramatically. Everyone prior to this had simply awaited his marching orders.

- Does he see himself as an individual "island" of contribution or as a member (or leader) of a team? Does she have a support structure or work in an isolated manner? Does he or she eat alone or with others?
- Does he have an objective and accurate assessment of the repercussions of his actions? Does she factually summarize what's occurred, or is she unduly pessimistic or optimistic?

If you're coaching someone who travels, then travel with the client. If the individual spends the day on the phone, then get a "y-jack" or sit on an extension, but spend the day hearing both sides of the conversation. If the client receives and responds to a ton of email, take a look at it yourself.

My experience is that you cannot do high-quality coaching over the phone. You can follow up over the phone and certainly offer situational guidance. But until and unless you've actually observed behavior in the workplace, you're in a poor position to offer remote help.

> *Ultimata:* The "rules of engagement" under which you both agree to interact will determine how rapidly and effectively you help the client. Don't make them up as you go along, or the client will do the same thing.

ESTABLISHING THE RULES OF ENGAGEMENT

Coaching is, perhaps, the most intimate and personal of all consulting assignments. Just as we try to avoid "scope creep" in large projects by establishing clear objectives to be met and joint accountabilities of client and consultant, we must clearly define the interactions and expectations of coaching.

Every project is different. But here is an example of some rules of engagement that might apply to virtually any coaching assignment—and to which you and the client must agree:

1. *Total candor at all times.* If the client is expecting just a pat on the head or a very soft critique, this is the time to disabuse her of that notion. Likewise, the consultant needs to be told if he is acting inappropriately or not providing useful feedback and guidance.
2. *Total confidentiality.* The feedback is for the client only. (This is a case, by the way, wherein even if the boss is paying for the assignment, the person being coached is the client.) You will not reveal anything you see or hear to anyone other than the client.
3. *Total access.* With the legitimate exception of certain confidential meetings, the client should not determine where and when he or she is observed. You must ensure random and unorchestrated observations.
4. *Periodic feedback at designated times.* Feedback should occur at set intervals (I advise at least at the conclusion of each shadowing experience, or once

a week), and appropriate time should be set aside for the feedback sessions. The consultant is obligated to provide two things: Specific behaviors and statements and specific recommendations for improvement when called for. The client is obligated to listen without defensiveness, to ask for clarification where needed, and to question whether a suggested approach will actually work.

5. *Clear results mileposts.* Since coaching often turns up needs and requirements unanticipated at the outset, it's helpful *during the process* to establish what the final improvement goals are and how they will be measured. This is important for disengaging successfully and determining whether or not the client is capable of the changes required. (It doesn't take six months to run a meeting better or to stop interrupting people.)

6. *Job performance aids as appropriate.* It's incumbent on the consultant to offer support and catalysts for the advice where appropriate. For example, someone always late and without time sensitivity needs a pragmatic calendar device to keep him or her on track. Someone who is a poor interviewer needs a list of behavioral interviewing questions to ask a job applicant. Volition is often insufficient. Your client will frequently need permanent job aids to assist in the requisite improvement areas.

Ultimata: Start with the expectation that everyone wants to improve. Allow yourself to be proved wrong if the client becomes defensive or resistant, but don't start the process with the philosophy that the client is somehow "damaged." Your client is probably doing most things right.

These (or similar) rules of engagement should be included in your proposal, with appropriate dates and specifics. It's not a bad idea to provide them on a plastic card or desk reminder to the client as well, so that you can both refer to them regularly. For example, I've had consultants complain to me that their coaching clients aren't returning their calls! That's an indication of a lack of any rules of engagement whatsoever. Coaching is not something you do "to" a client; it's a mutual pursuit that the two of you engage in to better the client's condition (and virtually always your own, as well, if you're a life-long learner).

There can be rules of engagement that are created post-coaching for the client and the organization as well.

Along with the rules of engagement, you might want to offer a questionnaire to learn as much as you can about your client in advance. There is no such instrument that is perfect, but here are some questions I've learned can generate a useful profile. Note that you can delve into personal details if you so choose.

Twenty Questions for Coaching Effectiveness
1. What is your educational background?
2. What was your work experience prior to this position?

CASE STUDY #14

I was coaching an executive who simply could not resist directly intervening with his subordinates' direct reports. In other words, he'd reach down two or three levels in the organization and provide direction, often countermanding his own subordinates' orders.

The rules of engagement we developed post-coaching and feedback included these:

- It's positive and powerful to be seen around the organization and to inquire about conditions, but you may not provide counsel or direction on any substantive issue without going through your own subordinates.

- You are never to question a subordinate's policies or procedures or judgment with anyone who works for him or her. Those questions are, however, properly directed at the subordinate personally.

- When you do believe you've seen something which requires attention, you should set a priority: If minor, wait for the next communication with the subordinate; if major, contact him or her or leave a message asking for an immediate response.

The subordinates were given the rules of engagement so that they could keep their boss "honest." It worked, although painfully at first.

3. Did you serve in the military and, if so, in what capacity?
4. What is your marital and family status?
5. What are your hobbies and interests?
6. To what professional associations do you belong?
7. To what civic or social organizations do you belong?
8. What were the last three books you read?
9. How often do you go on vacation, and where do you tend to go?
10. What percentage of the time do you travel on business?
11. How would you describe your current health?
12. Do you exercise or work out regularly and, if so, how?
13. What has been your proudest professional accomplishment?
14. What has been your greatest professional failure?
15. Ideally, what would you like to accomplish in the next year or two?
16. If you could change one thing about the job tomorrow, what would it be?
17. What would you do if you retired tomorrow?
18. What are your greatest professional strengths?
19. In what areas do you feel you need to improve professionally?
20. What is the best aspect of your life right now?

Ultimata: Always look for the simple explanations first (a principle often known philosophically as Occam's razor). Sometimes merely reducing hours on the job will erase a multitude of problems. Remember that you want to be corrective—remove the causes—and not merely adaptive—putting bandages on the hurt.

The clearer your rules of engagement at the outset, the more effective, more dramatic, and more quickly arrived at will be your results.

PROVIDING EFFECTIVE FEEDBACK

Unsolicited feedback isn't usually worth the breath taken to convey it, but solicited feedback is, by definition, highly valued. And the solicited feedback in a structured coaching relationship is, perhaps, the most useful, valuable, and potentially explosive of all.

Here are some rules of effective feedback, from coach to client, which ought to constitute your own "rules of engagement" for these projects.

1. Establish Dedicated Personal Time

Don't try to provide feedback "on the fly" or by email. Establish scheduled periods of undisturbed time when you can carefully explain your findings and the client can reflectively probe for clarification, examples, and help.

Unless the client is willing and able to insulate his or her office from distraction, phones, and assistants, it's a good idea to use a conference room somewhere else in the building. Meeting offsite also works, but don't attempt to provide feedback over a meal in a crowded restaurant or club. A private club, a private room, or a conference room after a meal all make sense. I've often had breakfast with a coaching client in a private room so that we're not taking time out of the day and the client can apply the techniques we discuss immediately on arrival in the office.

2. Provide Frequent Feedback

Especially at the outset, feedback less than once a week makes little sense in terms of creating the momentum for change and overcoming current inertia. If you must travel a great distance to reach the client, then provide a feedback session during every visit. If the client is within easy reach, then you have more flexibility.

The more time between feedback sessions, the more time for the wrong habits to continue to become ingrained. And the more time the client has to wonder whether he or she really needs you at all and whether this coaching "thing" really works.

3. Include Positives, but Don't Worry About "Balance"

I've seen coaches create performing seals among their clients. The bad news is always preceded (or followed) by good news. Do the trick and you'll get a fish.

By all means, provide the client with information about what's working well. That's only fair; it's important to reinforce good habits, and it adds to your credibility. But don't feel any obligation to create a balance of three pounds of good news to two pounds of bad news or some crazy sequence. Some clients need very little remedial work; some need to be totally reengineered. Honesty is more important than balance. Call 'em as you see 'em.

> *Ultimata:* Some clients can raise defensiveness to an art form. Call them on it immediately. Tell them that if they're perfect, you're not sure what you're doing there. Perhaps you should be coaching the other twenty people?

4. Cite Observed Behavior and Support It with Examples

Tell the client what you saw, what you heard, and how the client acted. Cite clear examples from your observations, for example, "When Harry told you the construction was delayed because of the contractor's error, you tried to call the contractor yourself rather than allow Harry to explain why he had decided to simply accept the delay."

Never engage in psychobabble ("I think your own background of poverty leads you to be overzealous guarding the company's money"). If you must, ask the client what her motive was ("When you refused to intervene in that argument, what were you thinking about?").[3]

You'll find that a client will be much more receptive, much less argumentative, and much more open to a remedial action when you cite and prove dysfunctional behavior in an objective, factual manner.

5. Be Prepared to Alternate Between Soft and Hard

On some occasions we have to gently persuade someone that an old, cherished behavior or habit has to go ("You can't call the women 'honey,' and you shouldn't be attending the sales meeting because they can't speak freely with you there"). On other occasions, we have to hit the client with a two-by-four

---

3. And never, ever, say, "Here's what I would have done. . . ."

Executives crave feedback (if they're any good) because they get precious little of it on the job from subordinates, peers, and superiors. Usually, customers are the only candid sources, and they are few and far between at executive levels.

I was working with the president of a $400 million division of a health care products organization. He was superb. Only about 10 percent of my feedback could be construed as "negative" or requiring improvement. Yet he kept asking me during each visit for harsher and harsher assessments.

This continued through our final debriefing at the end of the project. I finally had to tell him—in all honesty—that he was one of the finest, most powerful executives I had ever seen. We shook hands and I was headed for the door when he stopped me.

He knew that Merck, the pharmaceutical giant and annual "most admired" company, was one of my long-standing clients at the time. "Could I make it at this level within Merck?" he asked quietly. I assured him that he could.

We all have our doubts, including our powerful clients sitting in large offices counting their stock options. Underneath are quite often feet of clay. One of the great ironies of coaching is that we have to improve our clients' self-esteem more than anything else. That's done by pointing out what they do well.

("You've said three times that you want your people to be truthful, but twice today you 'whacked' people who simply told you an unpleasant truth").

You can often only help your client by creating some pain. Remember that your overall objective is positive and constructive change. It is not to engender harmony and good feelings at every step in that process. Particularly when you're dealing with tough leaders, you have to adopt a tough posture. If you let them intimidate you, ride over you, or shout you down, you have lost all effectiveness as a coach and might as well resign. You've simply allowed yourself to become another "yes man."

Ultimata: Deal forcefully with strong people. Deal gently with mild people. But sometimes temporarily reversing that flow will create rapt attention.

6. Set Up Monitoring Points and Progress Indicators

If you've reached agreement that meetings must be run more effectively, with a results agenda and clear decisions made on each item, then set up the next meeting as the first test and provide job aids (e.g., an agenda circulated in advance with the decision to be made) for that event.

If more effective performance evaluations or better interviewing techniques are the key, then provide the help and the aids and agree on observing at the next opportunity (preferably later that day, which is why I'm partial to breakfast debriefings).

Once the client sees progress and can appreciate the results of his or her changed behaviors, these will be reinforced and self-perpetuated.

Your feedback sessions may well become less frequent as the project unfolds. You should have a final debriefing at the conclusion. You might have provided documentation along the way. If you haven't, then there should be a written summary at the conclusion. (This will be extremely helpful should you be asked to coach that client again in the future.) At the final debriefing, emphasize the *major* points that the client should be focused on (e.g., contact customers once a week, interview people with behavioral questions, allow others to finish their sentences without interruption, and so on).

My preference is to allow for the client to continue to contact me remotely for at least three months. That means that phone calls, faxes, and emails are all welcomed, and I'll happily respond at the client's request even though the project is officially over. Requests from the client indicate a continuing intent to improve and may well cover some areas you were remiss in addressing during your time together. It's also a superb way to remain in contact and to further your business as a coach.

I believe that our obligation to provide constructive feedback doesn't end on a given date, although the formal mechanism might. These are intimate relationships which shouldn't simply be ruptured because payment has concluded.

If you maintain contact and encourage the client to do so, you'll find that coaching projects are among the most fulfilling of your career and also among the most lucrative in terms of referral business.

WHEN MORE THAN ONE COACH IS REQUIRED

If you coach long enough with a diversity of people, you will ineluctably run into a client who is definitely in need, but not of what you have to offer.

Not all problems are soluble through skills transfer, behavior modification, or even sheer volition. There are occasions when you will find personality disorders, emotional problems, and medical conditions that do require help, but that of a trained professional in those areas rather than of a consultant.

A brief word here to some of my brethren who, like me, also have psychological credentials: You cannot serve as both consultant or coach *and* therapist to the same client. You were brought in with a specific charter, and to suddenly switch to a new role is awkward at best and unethical at worst.

Why do I feel so strongly? Well, a consultant's job is to focus on observed behavior and to provide opinions, feedback, direction, and critique. It is, by necessity, a *judgmental* pursuit.

However, a therapist's job is to focus on underlying motivations, often rooted in nurturing and socialization factors, and to merely guide the patient (note that the subject is not a client, but a patient) toward self-discovery and self-awareness, often through deliberately traumatic and painful self-revelation. Therapists are *non-judgmental*, are usually asking "How do you feel?" and not "What do you think?," and will refrain from strong critique and direction. If you confuse the two roles, you confuse the person you are trying to help. Moreover, you will probably make a botch of both of them.

Ultimata: Most psychologists aren't very adept at quickly understanding another's underlying motivations, and they're trained to do it. Everyone acting in a coaching capacity needs to avoid this foray into the psyche at all costs. Otherwise, you should have your own head examined.

For the vast majority of readers, who are not psychologically trained or inclined, you should restrict yourself to coaching but understand the signals that something other than coaching is required. Combinations of the following factors (and the more that are in evidence, the more conclusive they are) will indicate psychological, emotional, and medical problems.

Fourteen Warning Signs of Personality, Emotional, and Medical Disorders

1. A fixation on others being "out to get them" when there is no evidence to support such claims
2. Obsessive behaviors, for example, insisting on reading all subordinates' incoming and outgoing mail, approving decisions that are rightly made several levels below, and so on
3. Severe fatigue for prolonged periods; falling asleep inappropriately on a regular basis
4. Irrational outbursts of anger without inclination to prevent or control them
5. An uncaring attitude about significant events, decisions, and plans
6. Deviant behavior in meetings, for example, shouting, walking out of the room abruptly, deliberate lateness, heavy sarcasm, and so forth
7. Unwillingness to trust others, even subordinates and colleagues
8. The belief that everyone, including customers, is trying to cheat or take advantage of him or her personally
9. Continuing "cognitive dissonance"—saying one thing ("Let's maximize sales this quarter") while doing another (withholding sales promotion literature and marketing efforts for no apparent reasons)
10. Deliberately lying on major issues on a consistent basis
11. Overt cheating and/or stealing, for example, encouraging people to take office equipment, recording fictitious client lunches
12. The expressed belief or behaviors that show rules apply to others but not to her, for example, demanding punctuality while always personally late or forbidding personal calls while making them himself
13. Long absences, either during the day or for days on end
14. Signs of substance abuse, for example, alcohol on the breath during business hours, glazed eyes, inability to focus, frequent trips to the rest rooms or other places of privacy

> Ultimata: Not everyone who acts outside of the mainstream is dys-
> functional. But people who consistently engage in deviant behavior
> usually require far more than mere management coaching.

Any one or two of those warning signs may be false alarms, but if you see three or more you can be increasingly confident that the behavioral problems which led to a call for coaching are being caused by factors that will not respond to coaching. In fact, coaching an alcoholic to better hide the condition and perform on the job is an unethical act, since the potential harm (hitting someone while driving out of the parking lot) is immense.

THE ILLNESS CALLED "DEPRESSION"

A few words about depression, which is an increasing problem in our complex society. It would greatly enhance your effectiveness to read a few chapters in any good psychological textbook about depression, its symptoms, and its treatment.[4] "Manic depression" is more properly called "bi-polar" and is marked by periods of intense "highs" and "lows" in energy and output. Depression is eminently treatable through therapy and drug regimens, but untreated can have devastating effects on the victim, family, colleagues, and others.

The telltale symptoms of depression include

- Loss of interest in areas and avocations in which one was formerly passionate
- A sense of hopelessness
- Periods of intense energy and periods of no energy
- Great fatigue, including falling asleep during the day
- Insomnia at night

---

4. I encourage you to read novelist William Styron's *Darkness Visible: A Descent into Madness* (Vintage, 1990), a moving account of his own decline into, and recovery from, depression.

I was working with the president of a division of a large bank. He was making errors in judgment completely inconsistent with his track record of success. Under normal conditions, he was a tough, almost unapproachable executive who placed equally high demands on himself and on his staff.

After he was highly resistant at three separate breakfast meetings offsite, I finally learned something of his personal life (had given up a life-long interest in golf, was having relationship problems with his wife, was letting the house—which he had vigorously maintained—deteriorate) and realized that there was at least a 90 percent probability that he was suffering from bi-polar depression.

When I confronted him by pointing out that the work problems he was experiencing might not be a reflection on his competence but rather a medical condition, he was sufficiently stunned to agree to a therapist's evaluation. My conclusions were validated, he was placed on appropriate medication, and he is highly successful once again today.

The bank's faith, his own courage when confronted, and my ability to realize that this was not a "coaching issue" were all required to provide a positive outcome. Great coaches have to be in a position to recognize that.

And, needless to say, my relationship with that bank and my client is today unassailable.

- Giving prized possessions away unexpectedly and often randomly
- Ruptured relationships with loved ones, often abruptly
- Periods of great intensity and focus followed by lack of both
- Feelings of personal helplessness and insufficiency
- Loss of confidence; unwillingness to accept positive reinforcement
- Family history of depression (it is usually hereditary)

If you notice several of these signs, seek professional help for the client from the proper source. Most of the time, people who are depressed don't realize it and don't admit to it when confronted. Remember, this is an illness which needs medical intervention.

> *Ultimata:* Great coaches know when *not* to coach as well as when to coach. Coaching is about the client's improvement, not about the coach's ego or personal success. Not all clients will be able to progress at the same rate, and a few won't be able to progress at all. Coaching is an intent, not a guarantee of results.

FINAL THOUGHT

Athletic coaches allow the players to play, intervening only when they can help an athlete improve on his or her own ability. Management coaching is fundamentally the same. There is no "perfect image" to which your client should adhere. Instead, you should both agree on pragmatic improvement goals, on how you will know when they are reached, and on when you will disengage. Clients are adults, responsible for their own actions. You're both better off if you leave slightly early rather than stay too long.

CHAPTER 5

Culture Change and Change Management

You Are Not *the Change Agent, No Matter What They're Paying You*

Some areas of client need are eternal, and the areas of culture change and organization development (OD) are two of them. Egyptian pyramid construction had to be radically reengineered once the Jewish slaves escaped across the Red Sea, and nothing much has obviated the need for change since.

There are two kinds of change, of course: There is the change that is thrust on the client from competitors, government, consumers, climate, environment, social mores, technology, new knowledge, perception, and a raft of other, often fickle, factors. Then there is change that is deliberately wrought, either to escape the doldrums or to magnificently raise the bar to a still higher championship altitude.

In any of those scenarios, there are going to be employees who need to change their behaviors, work habits, feedback loops, interactions, accountabilities, and so on. The *cause* of the change is of minor impact, although I'll note any distinctions among the treatment of reactive and proactive changes in the text. But change is change, usually no matter what the driver.

Finally, eschew the myth that people are reluctant to change. In fact, they change every day that there is a traffic blockage, a new customer request, a failed computer system, or a personal crisis. People are quite resilient and actually quite adept at change.

What people *do* tend to resist is ambiguity. One of the most elemental aspects of change management is to remove the ambiguity effectively. That applies to managers and executives more than to anyone else.

THE ELEMENTS OF "CULTURE"

Since "culture change" is often chanted as a single word, let's begin by removing some ambiguity here and establishing a working definition:

Culture is that set of beliefs which governs behavior.

There are organizational cultures, divisional cultures, sales cultures, and so on. That's because various organizational units (and charities, Little Leagues, non-profits, schools, and so on) all have basic beliefs which govern behavior.

In FedEx™ the culture is one of "get the package there as promised, no matter what," which explains the great stories about FedEx employees restarting plane engines in the air and prying open stuck drop boxes. In Hewlett-Packard the culture is "the HP Way," which is a high consensus, team-oriented, gender-blind, and color-blind environment. In some brokerage and investment houses the culture is one of harsh competition, with verbal abuse, profanity, and "victories" over colleagues.

Attitudes form beliefs, which are manifest in behaviors. Those behaviors—what the customer, the visitor, colleagues, and others actually see—is the prevailing culture.

Ultimata: Sometimes culture can be changed structurally, say by putting the manager out on the floor with customers. But usually, substantive change is created by affecting the belief systems of key people.

It's important to make this manifest when dealing with your buyer. "Cognitive dissonance" is the unequivocal foe of culture change. If management tells employees that customer service quality is the top priority, but rewards people based on the number of calls taken per hour, the organization is saying one thing and doing another. Call rates will go up, but service will deteriorate.

Checklist for Change

The most direct way to implement major change within organization structures is to follow this process or some variation of it:

1. *Identify the Behaviors Desired.* What is it the buyer specifically wants to see, feel, hear, and experience? Don't accept simply "a more congenial workplace," which could mean anything from cartoons on the walls to laughing at the boss's jokes. Better: "We want to establish a workplace in which people voluntarily come in early and/or stay late and go out of their way to help colleagues without management intervention."

2. *Establish the Exact Indicators of Success.* "I'll know it when I see it" works for the Supreme Court and pornography, but not for change management projects. Better: "I'll observe people at work already when I arrive at 8:30 or still at their desks when I leave at 5:30. There will be fewer demands for help directed at me since people are helping each other."

3. *Determine What the Current Encouragers and Discouragers Are.* Support and reinforce what is already in place and build more such encouragers as needed. This could range from management's public recognition of people helping colleagues to flex-time, which allows people to take compensatory time after they've stayed until 9 p.m. to get out a key proposal. If the managers themselves are only working a thirty-five-hour week, then that has to stop and they have to set the example. Remove the dampeners that frustrate the behavior you seek.

4. *Involve Employees in the Change.* No one likes arbitrary change, and ownership of change heightens commitment more than any other single factor. Tell people what's desired, ask them how best to achieve it, and make appropriate interventions. If employees tell you that security is needed for the parking lot for those who work late, or that private conference rooms are needed for group

meetings which can't be conducted in cubicles, then implement those changes.

5. Monitor and Refine. Nothing ever works exactly as planned. The flex-time might mean that clients on the other coast are not going to be able to reach a "live" person at certain times, so schedules will have to be adjusted to compensate. Or you might find that a person is taking such advantage of the system that she's arranged for everyone else to do her job. Make the necessary mid-course corrections.

6. Provide Your Client with a Permanent Management Tool. Since any consultant is going to leave eventually, the manager, sponsor, or buyer involved must be the person accountable for the enduring change. Provide that person with a template for overseeing. For example, you might have a weekly checklist with key indicators (all phones covered during all national working hours) that can be perused regularly to assure that nothing "slips."

Ultimata: If you have a change process as a consultant, you can help your client to better understand what is to happen and what his or her role must be. You'll also be able to gauge progress together.

The key to effective organizational change is to help the client through the ambiguity (see Figure 5.1). The current state is perfectly clear—people have been living it—and the future state is usually desirable—it's not hard to paint a positive picture of the future. But it's the *journey* that can be intimidating. If you have a change process, you can provide the lantern to light the way.

CREATING EXEMPLARS AND AVATARS

The single greatest factor in encouraging change that I know of is the exemplar. If people are told that customer quality is the path to success, but the people they see being promoted have sacrificed all pretense of quality to make their sales numbers, then ambitious people will do what they see, not what they're

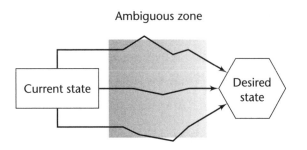

Ambiguous zone

Current state

Desired state

Figure 5.1. Moving Through the Ambiguous Zone with a Clear Change Process

CASE STUDY #17

The Federal Reserve Bank of New York was trying to improve its supervision of banks with an improved, although complex, matrix organization. They went about the change process about as well as I've ever observed.

The bank assigned a senior and respected vice president to head the change effort, with no other duties during that period. She created a variety of committees utilizing employees to provide information and ideas about the changes required and the impact on jobs and work procedures. The Fed hired an external consultant to "keep them honest" and critique the efficacy of the process as it progressed.

There were weekly updates via email and fax. There were "hot lines" to call for help. Focus groups were conducted weekly, both to gain more information about how to implement the changes and to assess reactions to current changes.

Finally, a six-month time frame was utilized, so as not to rush things and to provide time for the inevitable delays and fine-tuning. The new structure evolved into place with a minimum of disruption and an improvement in supervisory quality, according to the Fed management.

There was some unhappiness, which can never be avoided, an important lesson in change management. But the degree and scope were minimized.

told. Banners in the cafeteria lose all potency when opposite behavior is observed in meetings.

If avatars are so important, they had better be identified and reinforced before your major change efforts begin. Work with your buyer to determine the following:

- Who, by dint of hierarchical position, will be most effective as visible supporters (e.g., the vice president of marketing)? Note that these must be people whose behaviors can be seen by others on a regular basis.
- Who, by dint of respect, will be most effective as visible supporters (e.g., the five top-producing salespeople)?
- Who, by dint of expertise, will be most effective as visible supporters (e.g., a key customer experiencing the new process)?

Ultimata: There are virtually always people who can make or break a change management project by dint of their power and/or prestige. The best process will still fall prey to them. But a mediocre process can work wonders if supported by them. Think about what happens when you have a great process *and* their total support.

My approach to key sponsors is to be quite frank. I explain to them that the project's impact will hinge on their active support and involvement. My most powerful ploy is this one: *I try to minimize their work while maximizing their exposure.* In other words, I don't demand that they attend all team meetings, or put out memos, or visit twenty clients. But I do urge them to stand up at the company-wide meeting and express total support (which I will often script for them), to be interviewed by the house organ, and to never, ever undercut the program in even an off-handed or joking manner.

The converse of this dynamic occurs when you encounter (or are warned about) a key person who is the "anti-sponsor"—for whatever pure or impure motives, the person will try to undermine the project. When this occurs, never try to do battle yourself, because you'll be outgunned and outmaneuvered by someone who knows the terrain far better than you ever will. Instead, call in an air strike. Go to your buyer, point out the problem, and ask that one of two things occurs:

- The anti-sponsor changes to a positive supporter, under direct orders and threat from the boss. This can't be a slap on the wrist, but rather a facet in the person's annual evaluation. The person's self-interest must be tied to project success.
- The person is neutralized. The best way to do this is to remove the person by sending him or her on an international trip, providing a temporary assignment elsewhere, placing him or her on loan to a community group, asking the person to make an extended client tour, and so forth. By the time the person returns, the change should be in effect and too strongly rooted (and, one hopes, too popular) for him or her to undo.

Align your sponsors early, and make their accountabilities clear. Report to your buyer regularly about the sponsors' performance.

Ultimata: Remember that you are not the change agent. The client personnel are the change agents. You are the catalyst, but they are accountable for enduring change. Don't be a hero. Be a consultant.

Accountability is a key leverage point. I call this "post-heroic" change management, wherein you place the onus on the client and refuse to allow yourself to be the "easy out" for the client.

Figure 5.2 shows another method that can be used to dramatize to the client the need for the proper elements in the correct sequence, in this case beginning with hiring the right people.[1] In any change effort, the client must obtain the right people (hire or transfer), train them in the right elements

---

1. I call these "process visuals," and they are very effective for creating client commitment and removing ambiguity. A few are provided in Appendix A. An entire selection of them and recommended uses can be found in my book *The Great Big Book of Process Visuals, or Give Me a Double Axis Chart and I Can Rule the World* (Summit Consulting Group, Inc., 2000).

Figure 5.2. The Accountability Pyramid

and procedures, provide the right tools (e.g., technology), support them with recognition and reward, demand that they be accountable for the new direction, and monitor results. The role of the exemplar is especially critical at the support and accountability steps, no matter how strong the foundation.

It's worth spending a week or so to fully determine and appreciate who, exactly, can support your project over chasms and rifts and who can undermine it with a casual comment or stroke of the pen. This is a relationship business, and methodology is never enough (unless you consider these preventive actions as a part of your methodology).

Ultimata: Don't accept the client's statements as to who can help and who can hurt. Ask around. Observe meetings. Find out what's happened before. You're the objective observer, and you're likely to find more than merely meets the client's own eyes.

Many years ago my firm was running a project to improve innovation at the British Standards Institute outside of Milton Keynes in England. The culture change was immense, with the impact of the European Economic Community and increasing continental competition.

However, we were able to secure support, key sponsors, and the time needed. The internal teams responded grandly, and on a key final day to make plans to go forward, the managing director (CEO) attended for the first time. I had thought he was a figurehead off in London.

He listened to the plans for change and to become a leader in standards and testing in the new EEC. He then said this: "If these are such bloody good ideas, why haven't we thought of them before?" Then he left.

The project effectively collapsed. He was a venal, incompetent executive, but nonetheless, we should have pushed harder to determine his real power and prevent what happened.

REINFORCING CHANGE

I was conducting my first offsite strategy meeting with the senior management team of a new, high-tech client when one of the four owners suddenly shouted, "When can we expect the productivity problem to be corrected? We hired you as the change agent, and, after two months, not much has happened!"

He hadn't hired me, and he wasn't the buyer, so I felt I had to yell back: "*I'm* not the change agent, *you* are!" That stunned him into silence for a while.

On another occasion, while making a speech on change management at the American Press Institute, a reporter whose team had just won a Pulitzer Prize, and who therefore assumed he knew everything about everything, abruptly contributed this: "Just throw money at people and you'll get them to do anything you want them to!" I doubt that money is what kept him in journalism, which is among the poorest paying of professions, or that he's prouder of his W2 income statement than he is of his Pulitzer.

The *absence* of money is a demotivator, but its presence is not a motivator.[2] "Carrots and sticks" are not enough. If they were, we'd simply have a group of taskmasters sitting at the management desks (and, too often, we do!). Change agents are people on the job, in the environment, *accountable* for the business, who guide and nudge change every day. Consultants put the levers, cranks, pulleys, and pistons in place, but they can't be the ones who work the machinery.

As you can see in Figure 5.3, if you want to change behavior with carrots and sticks, you pretty much have to continue to provide the carrots on the new path and use the stick on those who insist on the old path. This doesn't work, it's expensive in terms of time and energy, and you don't need a consultant to tell you how to do this.

People change through only three factors, and two of them don't work:

1. *Power.* Managers attempt to change others through "orders," the threat of financial penalty, unfavorable assignments, or public ridicule. Power achieves temporary movement, but not commitment or motivation.

Ultimata: Ask yourself what prompts you to change for the long term. You're probably in consulting because you're a refugee from organizations which attempted to use power arbitrarily to affect your performance. The ultimate "stick" is termination.

---

2. *Normative or peer pressure.* The attempt here is to convince people to "be a part of the 'in' crowd." You might call it the "lemming approach." It, too, is short-lived and fickle, and gains compliance, not commitment.
3. *Rational self-interest.* In this case, the individual sees a fundamentally important reason for himself or herself to change (improvement, contribution, fulfillment, learning, and so on) and commits to it. This is the heart of motivation, which is always intrinsic, never externally "produced."

---

2. If you're dealing in organizational change and haven't read Frederick Herzberg and "hygiene theory," you should.

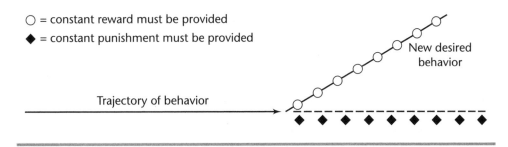

Figure 5.3. Why Rewards Aren't Sufficient

Hence, the true change agents are internal people whose self-interests are involved in the change *and who are able to affect the self-interests of others.* The near-legendary contemporary business leaders—Jack Welch at GE, Herb Kelleher at Southwest Airlines, Gordon Bethune at Continental Airlines, Lou Gerstner at IBM—have all had the capacity to embrace others within their own value systems, to touch people's most basic gratifications on the job, and to exemplify their intent for the organization.

THE REAL CHANGE AGENTS AT WORK

In creating culture change, we must put in place key organizational change agents who can appeal to others' self-interests. Too often we have managers telling their people, "Here's the latest fiasco" or "This is what the powers-that-be have demanded" or "That stupid consultant thinks we should be doing this."

Here's an example of a better way. When I began working with a large tele-marketing organization, I noticed that the people on the phones continually fell into poor habits (e.g., discussing price with the customer and caving in to demands for a lower price), no matter how effective the joint calls and role plays had been in training (e.g., turning the conversation to value and refusing to discuss price at the outset). The change agents—the consultants and trainers—were only present sporadically and often under artificial circumstances.

I realized that the problem was in having the wrong change agents at the wrong times. We moved the president of the division and the vice president of sales—both highly respected for their sales abilities in building the operation—to open desks on the sales floor. In that manner, they could hear the conversations going on around them, were constantly available for "real time" advice, and could contribute instantly. Within two weeks, the sales team had vastly improved its phone techniques, and after a month we could change the procedure so that the two executives each spent a separate day on the floor instead of the complete week (which helped to keep them apprised of what the sales team was facing and what was needed anyway).

Ultimata: Structural change supports performance change. Structural change never involves the consultant except for the design. You must alter the environment and the relationships to support the change that's required.

If you want to create organizational change, you must identify and prepare the organizational people who will lead, exemplify, and reinforce that change. If there's a type of sale which is no longer acceptable, then sales managers have to refuse to honor it when the field submits it. If customer service backlogs must be cleared, then managers must be visible working overtime to help the staff through the work. If repair people are to solve the problem during the first visit and avoid costly repeat visits, then equip them with the laptop computers they need and ensure that the repair manager appreciates the investment and supports it.

The changes you create at the beginning of the project are not the important ones. The changes that exist six months later and which endure are the important ones. Our value is in that enduring change—one that survives without the help of the consultant nurturing it regularly.

The only way that long-term change will take hold is through internal change agents regularly appealing to employees' rational self-interest. Carrots and sticks simply create an expectation of larger carrots and heavier sticks. (People are like sponges, in that they can absorb a nearly endless stream of rewards and can tolerate a lot more "pain" than one would expect if the pain of changing is even greater.)

One final point: The higher level, more visible, and more respected the change agents, the better. It's no accident that I used CEOs above as examples of great change agents. People do follow leaders whom they respect. That's not the consultant.

In a hospital client system, there were plaques on every available wall specifying the organization's value system. The fourth value listed was "We respect our people."

Yet the place was notorious for forced overtime, poor communications, arrogant doctors, insufficient staffing, and a raft of other obvious problems. It wasn't unusual, in fact, to observe managers berating people publicly, figuratively beating people right in front of these plaques on the walls!

The CEO corralled me one day shortly after I had begun work, and said, "I can't understand our morale problems. Our prior consultants worked with the executive team for weeks to develop and communicate our values, vision, and mission. How can we have so many subversive elements among our employee population?"

"Bill," I finally said, "do you think people believe what they read on the walls or what they see in the halls?"

OVERCOMING RESISTANCE

The key resistance to change will seldom come from employees, but will usually originate in other areas. The good news is that we know what these areas are. The bad news is that we often assume that nothing will go wrong once the brilliance of our design is appreciated.

> *Ultimata:* Assume that there will always be strong resistance to any change initiative—and from every possible source. If your preparations are unnecessary, you and the client are still better off than having been mugged by the unexpected resistance lurking in the halls.

You probably have your own favorite change "enemies," but here are the generic ones that I most frequently encounter.

1. The Compensation (or Reward) System

"We can't do this because the field is rewarded for other behaviors, and we can't possibly change the comp system in mid-year." This is the "Maginot Line" of resistance.[3] You must outflank it. Reward systems are designed to reinforce desirable behaviors, not to be themselves sacrosanct and preserved with sacrifices from the gods. A comp system can always be changed, modified, or superceded. How many times do you have the luxury of a project which can coincide with a new fiscal year and a change in comp plans from day one? Never.

Action: Design a transition comp plan, involve the people affected in the design, demonstrate the ultimate benefits of the new design, and have a very key sponsor take the position publicly that there is no option, as we are committed to the new path. Reward systems are inputs to performance, not outcomes themselves.

2. The Accounting System

Unbelievably, I've often been told that "We can't sell it at those amounts, because the accounting system can't report it that way." Former presidential candidate Eugene McCarthy said once, "Whatever is morally necessary must be made politically possible." Well, whatever is organizationally required must be supported by the infrastructure. Never allow a computer system, reporting mechanism, or logistical procedure to stand in the way of change.

Action: Recruit the key leaders in support functions involved early, and work with them to change the systems. *Beware:* They will often try to change your project to conform with their beloved systems. Use the leverage of your buyer to help move this in the right direction.

3. Unions

In some instances, union/management relations are so poor that a suggestion by the latter to reduce the work week at full pay would be opposed by the for-

---

3. For those of you deficient in history, the Maginot Line was a string of fortresses erected by the French after World War I in case of another war with Germany. It was supposedly impregnable. When World War II came, the Germans simply outflanked it and rendered it irrelevant.

mer just on the basis of the idea's origin. Unions can derail any project, and often management simply says, "Do whatever you can in spite of them." I'm of the opinion, however, that unions seek jobs at higher pay and completely understand productivity and quality needs. There are a lot of smart people over there who simply want to protect their interests. What's wrong with that?

Action: If a union's cooperation is key to the project, then reach out early and often. Involve both formal (officers) and informal (respected members) representatives. Demonstrate how the membership will be better off. Incorporate ideas. Even if the union isn't integral to success, involve the members anyway. Invariably, they are closest to the work and will have some of the best ideas for implementation.

Ultimata: If there were no resistance areas, why would the client need you? Don't be so surprised that they exist. Assume the worst and prepare for it. Sometimes the consultant is the first person who will "listen" to the rebels.

---

4. Vested Interests

I remember a sales director who realized that any realignment, no matter how necessary for the business, would jeopardize his hold on the top accounts in the company. He opposed every single plan for reorganization on the basis that the customers would not be served. His revenue stream was so powerful that he always carried the day. Finally, I convinced the buyer to allow a direct survey of the director's own customers, and we found that there was nearly zero vulnerability from the moves. The sales director was told that he had no choice (and resigned soon thereafter, realizing that he could never duplicate the revenues if he really had to work for them).

Action: Strike at the purported reasons that the vested interests use to prevent change. They are often the sole source of the "information," which is usually dubious, at best. You must demonstrate to the buyer that a single person's interests are being used to thwart those of the organization at large. (I once watched a cost reduction initiative stalled because a key vice president wanted to continue to fly first class. I told the president that the guy was making enough—over half a million—to afford the upgrade himself. End of story.)

5. Lethargy, Inertia, and Sloth

The sad but true fact is that many organizations and many managers are just too weary to make and support the requisite changes. They don't want to deal with the resistance of others (or the facts above), they doubt the value of the effort, they fear the risks, and so on. The point here is that if this is the way they perceive things, they're probably right! Never attempt to create accountabilities and plans with a disheartened or apathetic group. When the project fails, I guarantee that they won't be the ones who are blamed.

Action: It's incumbent on you to show a clear and positive risk/reward ratio. Prove to them—unequivocally—that the change will improve their lives (rational self-interest). You can make this very visible and analytical if you have to. See Figure 5.4 for an actual scale you can use to convince key people to support change aggressively.

When people have a clear idea of the reward versus the risk (of staying where they are and doing nothing), you can generally galvanize action, even among the previously exhausted.

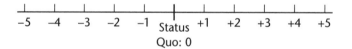

Question: What is the best and worst that might result?

+5 = Paradigm-breaking improvement, industry leader
+4 = Dramatic improvement, major publicity
+3 = Strong benefits, organization-wide
+2 = Minor benefits, localized
+1 = Very minor improvement, barely noticed

−1 = Very minor setback, barely noticed
−2 = Minor setback, controlled locally
−3 = Public setback, requires damage control
−4 = Major defeat, financial damages, recovery time needed
−5 = Devastating losses

Figure 5.4. Benefit in Relation to the Status Quo

My client was dithering about getting under way in a fit of false starts and real stops. Finally, I created a metaphor: Someone had to pull the trigger.

I explained that no one wanted to take the risk of leading the initiative, so everyone had a reason why it wouldn't work. On the other hand, no one wanted to be left behind by a successful initiative, so everyone had a reason why he or she should be involved. No one was pushing, no one was pulling, everyone was dead weight.

I told the buyer to get people to the starting line and pull the trigger on the starter's pistol. Whoever wanted to run the course the fastest would be the de facto leader. But the buyer would be watching to see who put in what kind of effort.

Once the decision was clear that the trigger would be pulled on June 1, people got in the starting blocks and came out running.

Ultimata: Remind people that it's their organization, not yours, and they will have to live with the ramifications of a failed project, lack of an improved condition, or opportunity wasted. If that's the place they want to work within, then why do they need you?

FINAL THOUGHT

Culture change is a matter of finding belief systems and altering them through enlightened self-interest. Support the change with structural reinforcement and onsite change agents. Then move to your next successful assignment.

CHAPTER 6

An Interlude: Managing Misfortune

*If You Can't Stand the Chaos,
Get Out of the Maelstrom*

Midway through this book I thought we ought to pause for some pragmatic reflection. Before we get carried away with the niceties of implementation, we should confront the fact that virtually no project proceeds the way we intended it to!

Human behavior and organizational vagaries are simply too complex and unpredictable to choreograph perfectly in advance. Consequently, no matter how rigorous your data gathering, despite the sincere commitment of your sponsors, and in spite of your world-class methodology, you're going to find the project delayed or diverted due to anything from a minor leak in the engine room to a torpedo in the bow.

So I thought we should have this "get real" moment and discuss everything from inadvertent error to outright stupidity (on the client's part or on yours). Ironically, most of us are prepared to be denied work (rejected) but not to lose work once it's begun (regurgitated). This is a chapter on how to set things right, where possible, and continue your work (rejuvenated).

Think back to those times when you were surprised, waylaid, unsaddled, and outright stopped at various points in a project. If you're at all like me, you don't have to think back very far. The more veteran and successful we are, the more complex and chaotic our clients and our work seem to be. That comes with the turf.

What follows below is some advice on how not be ground into that turf.

SCOPE CREEP DENIED

The most pernicious form of project problem that I encounter is that of "scope creep," a term I first heard while helping the consulting operation at Hewlett-Packard, but which seems to be a profession-wide expression. For the uninitiated: *Scope creep is that phenomenon which occurs when a client demands more and more services from the consultant, and the consultant keeps delivering them, thus progressively reducing the profitability of the project to the point of no return.*

My friends at HP, engaged in million-dollar projects, found that the implementing team was loath to reject any client request—even from low-level client personnel—because of the fear of endangering the project. So they agreed to virtually every client request ("Say, as long as you're here, can we reprogram this parallel system?"), thereby endangering the project. These concessions were called "undocumented promises," meaning that they weren't contractual and weren't included in the proposal or contract, but they were formally expected by the client since someone at HP had said, "Sure."

Ultimata: The most important aspect of any project are the objectives. They constitute a template for the client to use to judge progress and value and a template for the consultant to use to restrict project scope.

The hair on my neck stands at attention when a client begins a sentence with "As long as you're here . . ." or "I thought if you had the . . ." or "Here's something else I'd like your opinion on." Now, I'm a big believer in expanding business and in providing value to induce clients to expand business, but here's the difference: *Giving a brief opinion, suggesting a course of action, and providing feedback are harmless, additional value-added components. But creating a formal plan, implementing a solution, investigating a condition, and making dedicated trips for an issue fall into the realm of CASC (consultant-aided scope creep).*

Scope creep is seldom malicious. It occurs through the client's best intentions and self-interests and the consultant's vacillation, ambiguity, and fear. Here are the main causes.

The Ten Creepy Causes of Scope Creep

1. When the consultant bills by the hour or day, the client reasonably expects to want to "use" that time, so why not ask that other things be done if the visit's primary objectives have been met but there's still time on the clock? (I once heard a professional speaker say that he was simply a "hired hand" onsite and would move the furniture as long as he was being paid to be there. In which case he wasn't a speaker, but a handyman.)
2. The buyer truly respects the consultant and wants to involve the consultant in as many key issues as possible.
3. The buyer believes that there are, indeed, ancillary and peripheral issues which affect the project and must be addressed.
4. Information comes to light after the initial engagement that the client believes is an integral part of the engagement (e.g., the turnover is caused by the non-competitive compensation system, and that system needs an interim improvement immediately).
5. Events occur which affect the project (e.g., the sales vice president is recruited away and that department needs guidance until a replacement can be found, which will take at least ninety days).
6. The consultant is afraid of endangering the business and is fearful of rejecting a request or suggesting that it constitutes a new project.
7. Client personnel see the consultant as a peer and/or another implementer and use the consultant as a contract employee when he or she is present.
8. The buyer's boss enters the picture with additional "suggestions" (AKA demands).

9. The consultant has made a mistake, vastly underestimating the contributing factors which cause the condition or prevent its removal (e.g., it's a supplier problem as well, not just an internal one).

10. The consultant's ego runs amok, and early successes lead him or her to begin attacking all problems as though the one portion of the kitchen floor that has been polished now makes the rest of the room look dingy.

Ultimata: Scope creep cannot occur—can not occur—without the active participation of both the client and the consultant. By simply ending your participation unilaterally, you end scope creep. It's that simple.

TWO LINES OF DEFENSE

The best time to prevent scope creep is before you begin. Create clear, lucid, crisp, *and agreed on* objectives in the proposal, which the buyer signs off on. If you have a coaching client and the objective is "to improve Jane Withers as a manager and leader," then she can rightfully expect from you anything from improving meeting and presentation skills to enhanced decision making and strategic planning abilities. But if the objective is "to improve Jane Withers' ability to establish growth strategies that her unit can achieve," then the former competencies are out of the picture.

Similarly, the objective for the Acme Company to "improve competitive position in the marketplace" can encompass public image, competitive intelligence, better hiring, product cycle time, and a plethora of factors. But the objective to "create better brand awareness for Acme among forty-five- to fifty-five-year-old buyers" provides for a rather circumscribed branding campaign.[1]

---

1. And note that, even here, branding may include advertising, sponsorships, promotions, publishing, endorsements, and so on. On the other hand, the objective, "Create better brand awareness among forty-five- to fifty-five-year-old buyers through lifestyle endorsements" provides for even narrower project scope.

My buyer at the Federal Reserve Bank asked if I would chat with a person newly appointed to oversee knowledge management within the organization and let her know what I thought of the initiative. I readily agreed and spent an hour with the woman in question during a normal visit to the site.

At the end of the day, the buyer asked me if it had gone well and what would likely happen next. I said that it had gone very well, and that what happened next was up to her. She asked what I meant.

"Well, if you want me to touch base with her occasionally when I'm here and have the time, I'm happy to do that. The drawback is that we're probably not going to match up well, either in terms of schedule or her practical needs. However, if you'd like me to establish some objectives for progress with her and create a schedule to ensure we both work on it systematically, I'm happy to do that. But that's a new project, and I'll have to present you with a new proposal. That's the only way to do justice to you and her, fairly."

The buyer was appreciative, but asked that I simply focus on the existing, critical project. That ended the requests and ensured that I wasn't lured into more work at no pay.

The second weapon against scope creep—after ensuring that your initial objectives are limited—is to push back when you're asked. Once again, providing some "free" value by sticking your toe in the water is one thing on a restricted basis, but wading into the swamp is quite another.

You must be confident enough to tell the client that you're being asked to do something that is not in keeping with your contract (and this will work even with oral agreements reached among long-time buyers). Don't reject the request (if it's within your competency), but simply deflect it by explaining that *to do the client organization justice* you will have to create a new plan and new proposal to embrace the additional work. That's the win/win proposition.

> *Ultimata:* The key to pushing back against scope creep is to convince the buyer that it's in his or her best interests to view the suggested new work as an additional project. It's not a matter of your work load; it's a matter of the quality of client results.

Demonstrate to the buyer that

- The work requires a separate and dedicated focus, not a "catch as catch can" approach
- You may need to call on separate resources, subcontractors, and so forth
- Different sponsors, implementers, and/or customers are involved
- While interrelated, the success of one is not dependent on the other
- Things will be clearer, more defined, and more quickly achieved with two discrete projects rather than one with a "poor cousin"

Scope creep is eminently preventable, since you alone are able to stop it. If you don't do so, it's not the client's fault. But it is your loss.

UNFORESEEN DRAMATIC EVENTS

I would assume that 95 percent of the people reading this book know immediately what I'm talking about. It's the equivalent of the boxer who is in command of the fight until the opponent lands a looping right hook that comes out of the rafters (or, perhaps more descriptive of some of my own knocks, as if the referee is suddenly no longer neutral, but takes a shot at you himself!).

I use the term "dramatic" because the events are usually a shock to both buyer and consultant (if not, then the buyer has been holding out on you and the relationship is not what it ought to be).

Key dramatic events include phenomena such as these:

- Divestiture, acquisition, or merger
- Management shakeup at significant levels

The CEO of Mallinckrodt's animal health subsidiary called me into his office one day, interrupting a planned visit with several of his subordinates. We had been working together for about a year on teamwork and operating efficiencies and had had sufficient progress so that the project was renewed to extend to additional areas.

"Alan," he said somberly, "I don't know how else to put it. We're being divested, and the word will be out by the end of the week. The parent is actively seeking buyers."

"Well, then let's get moving on how to tell the employees and on how to keep people from jumping ship," I said. "I've been through this before with Calgon and Merck's AgVet division, and part of the value of the sale will depend on the number and quality of key people who remain."

"Where do we start?" he said. And so we started right there.

- Removal of the buyer
- Competitive strike which has dire consequences
- Key talent defection or loss
- Profound change in earnings or other important results
- Adverse, widespread publicity over image, quality, and so on
- Major lawsuit
- Dramatic technological breakthrough or failure
- Economic collapse in one or more markets
- Significant management error (e.g., bad risk accepted in insurance)
- Critical customer or client losses

Ultimata: Dramatic events demand dramatic reactions. This isn't about scope creep. It's about changing the scope of the project to tackle the new developments. You can't continue to improve the menu diversity when the roof has collapsed on the dining room.

When such dramatic events intervene, you must dramatically change the nature of your project. This doesn't mean that you are violating the guidelines about scope creep. You're not enlarging the project; you're changing the project. (The alternative is to be deemed superfluous in the light of new events and to be thrown out, usually unpaid.)

One of the great advantages of being paid in advance (if you've read my other books on that subject) is that you represent an existing resource in the midst of chaos, not a bleeding wound. The client might as well use you, since you've already been paid and have expertise. If you haven't been fully paid at the point that bedlam breaks, then make that case forcefully. After all, you've come to know the company, you have the time allocated in your schedule, you may well have seen similar situations before, and the buyer trusts you (or you wouldn't be there to begin with).

Given all of that, how can the client *not* use you when every key resource needs to be addressed to the new problem? Here are some tactics to employ when all hell suddenly breaks loose.

Six Ways to Control Chaos

1. Get to your buyer, no matter by what means. (Which is why having his or her home phone number is always a good idea.) Establish contact and learn the nature of the issues that have arisen. (If your buyer is the one who's gone, contact the buyer's superior.)
2. Immediately present any experiences you've had which address the new developments, and provide options about how you can help.
3. Reach agreement that the current project is hereby in abeyance and that the new challenges must be met first. Make it clear, however, that the client's investment is now in the new focus and that the one being shelved will require further consideration if and when revived.
4. Don't be greedy. If the new requirements somewhat exceed the old ones, provide the help anyway. You'll be in better shape when it all ends. The client should continue to pay expenses, so even increased travel shouldn't be a problem.
5. Quickly introduce a tentative plan of action which relies on your help. The ability to make order out of unstructured and chaotic situations is a highly valuable asset.

> *Ultimata:* You must be forceful and aggressive when unexpected events turn conditions upside down. The passive and retiring will fall through the cracks, which will have become fissures.

6. Get started as soon as possible, no matter how minor the new intervention at the beginning. This quickly establishes you as part of the rescue operation instead of the scenery. (For example, if two key vice presidents depart for the competition, suggest that you coach their direct subordinates to serve as acting chiefs, that you investigate for other possible defections, or that you create a counter plan to attract talent, and so forth.)

Unforeseen dramatic events occur regularly, because no one is so smart as to always anticipate them and because business is getting so complex as to make them inevitable. A good consultant is actually "ready for the unforeseen."

SABOTAGE

While refraining from complete paranoia, many of us can point to projects that were deliberately sabotaged to crash and burn with our reputations (and perhaps unpaid invoices) consumed in the flames. It is rare, but it happens to the best of us.

Few people—even powerful executives—will take the risk of openly and aggressively sabotaging another executive's pet project, but many will just as effectively stop the parade through the organizational equivalent of passive-aggressive behavior. The worst thing that can befall us is the invalid assumption that all is going according to plan and people are living up to their commitments when, in truth, the wheels have come off.

It is the resistant client employees who are *not* aggressively opposed, who do *not* voice reservations, and who do *not* resist their accountabilities who are the most dangerous saboteurs. You must identify them early and confront the behavior as soon as possible. In most cases it's much more pleasant and less stressful for the consultant to simply "hang with" the people who support him or her and overtly back the project. But that's the path to minimum stress and maximum failure. You must wade in to the swamp, because that peculiar rock is actually the nostrils of an alligator.

Here are some tips on identifying, preventing, and dealing with sabotage.

Ten Ways to Identify Potential Sabotage

1. Are there people who were vehemently opposed to the project prior to your assignment or who were opposed to your receiving the assignment?
2. Will a department or division clearly be a net loser as a result of the project (e.g., fewer people, relocation, lowered pay scales, and so forth)?
3. Has this type of project failed in the past due to internal resistance?
4. Are there absolutely critical potential sponsors who refuse to attend meetings, support the initiative, or even return your calls?
5. Has a major portion of the population refused to participate (e.g., "Sales says that they'll produce their own customer surveys")?

Ultimata: Sabotage can occur at any time, but it's far more likely to take place quickly, before early successes can swing momentum (and fence sitters) in your favor and before you have the lay of the land.

6. Does your buyer tell you that "this will be a mandate from above, and everyone will be forced to participate"?
7. Are scheduled meetings and key events cancelled on short notice with no justification?
8. Is it difficult to secure key resources and access, even though the importance of their involvement was stressed at the outset?
9. Do people attempt to change the objectives of the project continually?
10. Are you falling behind schedule almost immediately?

Any one of these indicators doesn't necessarily mean that you've stepped on a land mine, but the presence of several almost ineluctably suggests that there is "incoming" artillery fire. Most of my projects don't have even one of these factors present, so when two or more surface, it may be time to go into preventive actions.

The indicators mean that resistance is under way, but it's probably too early to have done any real harm. Below are the effective preventive actions to blunt the opposition and insulate your project. (They don't apply one-to-one to the indicators, since any one preventive action can prevent several differing problems.)

Ten Steps to Prevent Potential Sabotage

1. *Have "zero tolerance" for any lateness or missed commitments.* Remind the parties involved and immediately inform your buyer. Don't let the foot dragging take root.
2. *Confront the dilatory parties.* If you can't arrange a meeting, ask your buyer to set one up. It's much harder to resist someone you've met face-to-face, and that tête-à-tête may just cause him or her to back down.
3. *Gather the most powerful sponsors on your side.* That includes hierarchical power as well as informal power (e.g., union leaders or top sales reps). Don't allow this to be a "them against you" battle.
4. *Document the problems.* Demonstrate to the buyer the nature and origins. Show any patterns that are developing ("Everyone has contributed except the finance department, and your CFO won't return my calls").
5. *Try to create a "win/win."* If a unit is, indeed, getting the short end of the stick, try to provide something of value. If pay scales will be reduced, offer a streamlined route to transfer to another division.
6. *Demonstrate early success.* There's nothing like a few, small, early "victories" to show people that the project works, makes sense, and will proceed no matter what.
7. *Communicate like crazy.* The grapevine is always working overtime, and its default setting is usually in the saboteurs' favor. Provide frequent updates on how things are going and how they're going well.

Ultimata: Consultants are sometimes called in to be beaten up and blamed for conditions which management has created and can't themselves correct. Even if you get paid, the repute and notoriety will linger. No matter how good your methodology, none if it includes walking on water.

8. *Everything starts with your buyer.* If he or she is on board and strongly supportive, you're still holding the ace. But if the buyer "disappears" by relegating you to subordinates, you just might be sabotaged from above. (Consultants are often brought in as the "fall guy.")

9. *Get paid in advance.* Organizations are much more prone to support someone who already has their money and hasn't yet completed the work than someone who can merely be cut adrift next week at no expense.

10. *Set very clear, crisp objectives.* And don't accept the work at all if you see a pattern of past defeats or a lack of support. The only thing worse than no business is bad business.

If the saboteurs have begun to take their toll, you're at a disadvantage and losing headway, but you're not dead in the water. The essential strategy at this point is simply not to go down with the ship. As John Paul Jones shouted over to the *Serapis,* as his own ship was sinking, "I have not yet begun to fight." He sailed home in the *Serapis,* as its captain.

Here are some tactics which still might help.

> *Ultimata:* This isn't about "getting even." It's about helping the buyer and, by extension, the client. If you don't make it personal, you won't make it so threatening to yourself.

Five Tactics for Dealing with Sabotage

1. *Focus only on observed behavior and objective evidence.* Don't confront someone with "You've been trying to undermine this project from the outset," but rather, "You haven't held one of the employee meetings you've promised to hold, and your people are not participating in the focus groups." Don't attempt to psychoanalyze; just describe the facts.

2. *Don't let your ego overrule your common sense or your emotion undermine your logic.* This isn't about you, per se; it's about some feared result or perceived diminished status. Don't take it personally or you'll be completely ineffective. The good of the buyer is at stake, not your own future.

The founder of the company had sold it to a Fortune 50 giant and left. His son remained as an executive vice president, now reporting to a president installed by the new parent. The son, Ronnie, was a monster, abusing employees, undercutting colleagues, and creating havoc wherever he went. The new executives brought me in to "coach" Ronnie, after themselves failing to correct his abysmal behavior over the course of a year.

Ronnie was all too happy to have me until after our first meeting, when he found out that I couldn't be "snowed" and I confronted him with near-legendary examples of his abusive behavior. After that, he was no longer available, complained about my professionalism, and contracted with his own private coach, flown in from across the country, to confirm that he was absolutely fine and more stable than all the rest of us.

Despite my having been paid, my contract was ended on the basis that my evaluation was incorrect and that I couldn't get along with Ronnie. Last I heard, he hadn't changed a whit, but the management could now say that he had had every possible type of support and it was no longer an issue.

I have not worked for that division—once a very good client—since.

---

3. *Always keep the client's improvement in mind.* You can shame people into changing their intransigence by pointing out *not* that you are being undermined, but that the organization's progress is being seriously delayed.

4. *Document everything of factual nature.* Include conversations and relay it all to the buyer. You and the buyer are collaborators, after all, and he or she has the key stake. Let the buyer know in no uncertain terms that the project is being scuttled and how that's happening.

5. *Stop, if you must.* Don't attempt to hold back a burst dam. If the forces allied against you are too strong or wily to overcome—which can often be the case with entrenched resistance to an "outsider"—then tell the buyer you can't continue without dramatic corporate intervention. You can't always be a hero, but you shouldn't be a martyr either.

I was trying to implement a new approach to customer service in a call center for a catalog and retail client. Service was slow and erratic, and the "failure work" caused by sloppiness was very expensive. There was virtually no extended selling going on over the phones.

My plans were quickly unraveled by two supervisors who had run the place for ten years under a manager who was largely absentee and totally uninterested. My client was his boss, the vice president.

Every attempt to train, provide job aids, and monitor calls was diverted and deflected. The supervisors were even spreading stories that I was there to downsize the operation. I finally went to the vice president and told him that what we were really facing was a reorganization, or my departure. He was shocked by my documented reports of the supervisors' actions.

The manager was transferred and the unit was placed under another area. Both supervisors were asked to resign, which they did, with early retirement packages. I felt no regret. The unit was running on all cylinders within ninety days.

Ultimata: If you've consulted with major organizations on key projects for more than five years and never failed, then you've either never taken on a tough challenge or you have failed and just don't realize it. With high-end, sophisticated consulting, occasional failure comes with the turf.

UGH! FAILURE!!

It happens to all of us. Sometimes we blow it. In twenty-six years of consulting (I began when I was twelve), I can readily recall half a dozen grade-A, certified, full-tilt, road-kill failures. In my estimation, here are the major causes of my irregular demise:

- *A belief that I could walk on water, and the commensurate refusal to set reasonable objectives which could be achieved within that client's culture, environment, and management structure.* The management wouldn't embrace and couldn't really understand the changes that I had in mind. My fault. I knew they were there.

- *A dumb accommodation of a new buyer in a new position to accept her plan instead of telling her it made no sense.* I should have pushed back immediately and vehemently, but I saw the potential for a long-term project and simply tried to be another "yes man." And, yes, I was the man who failed dismally. What she wanted couldn't be done.

- *Becoming so infatuated with my relationship with the CEO that it became the two of us against "them."* Once I was seen as nothing more than "the president's gunslinger," no one was honest or forthcoming, or even very cordial. My original ability to gather information and to be trusted with bottom-up comments evaporated. I got too comfortable in the executive suite.

- *Insufficiently developing relationships and trust with key people around the organization.* For example, the CFO was peripheral to my work, so I simply accepted an arm's-length relationship. But when the numbers and the forecasts became critical, there was no time to build up the requisite trust and I was left holding a gun that had no ammunition.

- *Sarcasm and insensitive approaches.* I had found quite unimpeachable evidence of the problem and the culprits, but I approached them like the wrath of God instead of with help and suggestions. I was too anxious to move too fast to please the buyer. Speed of change never outruns quality of change.

Ultimata: I've made quite a few mistakes finding my own way in this business, but never the same one twice. If you read these pages carefully, you don't even have to make mine once. It's not in avoiding mistakes; it's in avoiding *repeating* mistakes.

We all eventually find misfortune in this business. But we can do a lot to prevent it and still more to deal with it when it arises. Consulting, after all, is about success, not about perfection.

FINAL THOUGHT

Create a mastermind group with consultants you don't normally see for other purposes. Meet two or three times a year. But don't focus on "best practices" or "benchmarking." Focus on the group's mistakes, with the intent that you'll now be able to avoid those of another four or five very talented people. At West Point they spend far more time studying defeats than they do studying victories.

CHAPTER 7

Learning Lessons

Creating Dynamic Instruction

Many of you spend time in front of a classroom at one time or another. It may be something as formal as seminar training, or as impromptu as quickly transferring some skills to a customer service team in a time of crisis. But no matter what the reason, I've run into very few consultants who, over the course of a successful career, have not been involved in "platform" work.[1]

There's another kind of instruction as well, which occurs every time we're with a client. We are virtually always providing insights, help, encouragement, tactics, options, and direction one-on-one or with small, informal groups. This is no less an instructional environment, requiring an understanding of how people learn, how instruction becomes institutionalized, and when transference is effective.

---

1. In the speaking business, most people who actually make money are doing workshop and seminar training. There are relatively few of the more "glamorous" keynoters, but legions of in-the-trenches, hard-working classroom trainers.

There is an ancient platitude which holds that those who can, do; those who can't, teach (to which I added in *Million Dollar Consulting*, those who can't teach, consult). But teaching is an ancient and most honorable profession, one that was admired when medical people were considered nothing more than charlatans. The Romans admired the Greeks for their ability to instruct, and it is only quite recently, in the precarious and arbitrary economic priorities of post-Cold-War America, that the teaching profession has fallen on such hard times and low esteem.

Instructing is noble work, and we engage in it daily. Consequently, as consultants, we might as well get good at it.

LEARNING OBJECTIVES AS OUTCOMES

Let me state immediately that there is no better resource to learn about learning in the business environment than Bob Mager. You'll find the particulars in Appendix B, but simply read any of his wonderfully humorous and highly pragmatic works. My favorite is *Analyzing Performance Problems, or You Really Oughta Wanna*.

No training for formal instruction of any kind should ever take place without a clear learning objective, which is in turn based on a behavioral change that can be measured and that influences performance. (And such outcome-based expectations are not a bad idea for informal meetings, either. So many meetings are such a waste of so much time precisely because the consultant has not established what is expected to change as a result of the interaction.)

Ultimata: If you want to reduce client meetings, increase objectives and communicate them. If you don't know what changed behavior you're trying to achieve, how do you know when the meeting is over?

The overly specific (a task) and the overly general (a vague notion) should be equally avoided. Here are some examples of what I mean:

Too narrow: Teach employees to operate the new contact management system, including all recall functions, file sharing, Internet connectivity, and routine updates.

Too broad: Improve the ability to follow up with prospects.

On target: Participants will be able to use contact management software to set priorities on leads and follow up with all "A" category leads within ten days of first contact without duplication and with zero omissions.

Too narrow: Teach salespeople to use templates of questions to qualify buyers and achieve one of three possible positive choices at the conclusion of the first meeting.

Too broad: Improve sales close rate.

On target: Participants will be able to use basic consultative selling techniques to qualify buyer, ascertain budget, establish objectives, and gain permission to submit a proposal based on those objectives within thirty days of first contact 80 percent of the time.

Never run a "feel good" session. Even if your intent is to help employees to feel better about the new organizational structure, your learning objective might be: "Participants will understand the new reporting relationships and accountabilities to the extent that they can immediately call for the proper assistance or support without going through their supervisors or delaying the work until a later time. There will be zero work backlog at the end of a normal work day."

When you find yourself engaged in classroom training or formal skills transfer of any type, establish the following with your buyer:

- What are people expected to do differently as a result of this training?
- To what degree are they expected to do it differently?
- When should they be doing it differently, and with what consistency?
- How will you know they are performing as desired?
- How will they know they are performing as desired?
- How will you and I know that the skills transfer has been effective?

If you can answer these questions and gain the buyer's commitment to the answers, you have an effective training intervention. Another way to view the relationship between training and organizational development can be seen in Figure 7.1.

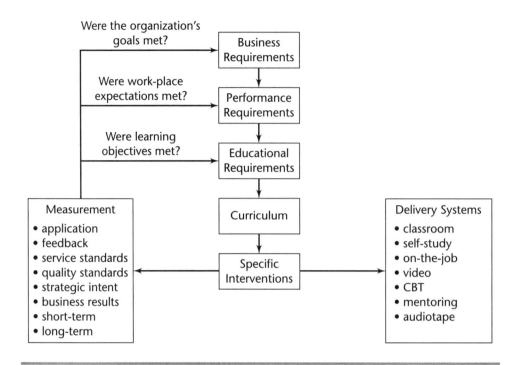

Figure 7.1. Organizational Education Tied to Strategic Goals

The chart illustrates that learning objectives and the chosen intervention really flow from ultimate performance goals. If you work "backwards" (or down the chart), you will always closely link learning with performance. However, if you work from the bottom up, you'll wind up with training programs poised to be solutions but actually in search of problems.

Ultimata: If training does not improve performance to the extent that it is recognized by the customer, I can make a case that it is irrelevant. In fact, this is why so much "quality" training is irrelevant. The customer neither sees nor perceives it.

I had been consistently the highest rated instructor on the faculty at GTE's corporate university. The human resource department, which ran the university, in a fit of quality zealotry, decided to provide a "quality guarantee." This meant that if a sufficient number of participants did not rate the program highly enough, the instructor's fee would be reduced, ultimately to zero.

Although I was in no danger, I told the vice president of HR that the plan was stupid and silly. The participants are the worst people to ask to evaluate a course. In fact, their bosses should be asked about a month later if there were any behavioral changes on the job consistent with the performance objectives of the instructional experience. Under the new plan, faculty would focus on being liked, not on being effective, and on "smile sheets" (ratings forms), rather than on workplace change.

GTE's human resource gurus made the only decision they could within their quality mindsets: They asked me not to come back. After all, I was not a team player.

It was one of the most enjoyable firings I've ever had. The faculty went on to record-setting testimonials, and GTE's performance continued to decline.

Training and development is rarely effectively measured (for reasons we'll examine later in this chapter) and therefore seldom truly appreciated, and consequently never properly funded (viz.: the fees are far too paltry). By connecting training to behavioral and performance outcomes needed to improve the business, the value and commensurate support can be turbocharged.

THE ADULT LEARNING SEQUENCE

For all you hear about "accelerated learning," or optimal learning conditions, or reinforced feedback, or the rest of the jargon, adults basically learn best in this sequence.

1. Discussion About the Improved Performance, Skills, and Outcomes Desired.   This includes *why* the change is necessary. Many authorities like to point out that training involves the "how," but true education involves the "why." The poet Maya Angelou has cleverly described how we train animals, but educate people. Without putting too much of a metaphysical spin on the issue, I have found that commitment to change only occurs when the people who must change understand why it is important to do so and how it is in their self-interest. Otherwise, you have compliance but not commitment. So the discussion step involves both the "why" and the "how," the reasons and the skill sets.

Ultimata: If people don't understand *why* they are doing something, they may master the rote but never the reason, meaning that they will be unable to use judgment and initiative when ambiguity arises. It's like the children who sing "The Sleigh Ride Song" with the lyrics "one horse soap anslay" rather than "one horse open sleigh." They can sing the tune, but have no idea what the lyrics mean.

---

2. Practice in a Safe Environment.   No one should learn to swim in the middle of the Pacific Ocean, and no one begins a singing career with the main aria from *Aida* at La Scala. Every key aspect of the new behavior should be practiced via role play, simulation, case study, small group exercise, demonstration, or other means—as many times as is necessary for that individual to achieve mastery. (This is what Mager calls self-paced, criterion-based instruction.) The police force might only give a morning overview of the difficulties expected on the officers' daily shift, but it makes sure that each one of them has fired a gun successfully, competently, and above minimal standards on a firing range periodically.

3. Feedback About How Well the Practice Was Performed.   Practice is useless in a vacuum. There is no such thing as "negative" or "positive" feedback in learning practice sessions. There is only objective feedback: the actual results and outcomes of the individual's performance. That's why flight simulators are prepared to provide both successful landings and fiery crashes. A pilot who crashes in the simulator doesn't emerge saying that the machine gave him or her negative feedback. The pilot says, "I blew it, and I have to improve that landing." It's somewhat better to do it there than in a real 747 at full throttle approaching O'Hare.

4. Application of the Skills on the Job. No practice or simulation can ever totally replicate actual job conditions, with the distractions, environment, and uncertainties of the workplace. No instruction, therefore, is really complete until the new behaviors are successfully *and consistently* demonstrated in the workplace. (This, by the way, is why consultants are superior investments to those who are solely trainers or HR people, because the classroom is always, by definition, insufficient to achieve effective application on the job.) Application involves the monitoring, coaching, and fine-tuning needed to ensure that the new behaviors are successfully implemented in the real world.

Ultimata: Positive behaviors need reinforcement and negative behaviors need discouragement. If you do neither, you will default to a third mechanism: the path of least resistance.

These four steps—discussion, practice, feedback, and application—represent the effective adult learning sequence. But I'll add one more, because it is unique to our particular value as consultants: reinforcement.

Once on the job, there is a fifth need. Although not technically part of the adult learning sequence, it is an integral part of effective consulting implementation, so it makes sense to note it here.

5. Reinforcement Both to Encourage the Newly Learned Behaviors and to Discourage Counter-Behaviors. This is where we really shine as consultants, although too few of us follow through as thoroughly as we should. Effective reinforcement should include *at least* an audit of the following:

- *Feedback loops.* The employee should be able to obtain feedback continually as to how well he or she is performing. This may include daily management feedback, objective indices (e.g., number of calls), regular customer feedback (many banks and hotels encourage immediate feedback from customers, often in return for a small reward), performance evaluations, and peer review.

- *Proper reward.* You shouldn't reward for number of sales calls made during a day if the behavior desired is customer satisfaction or total cross-selling of the full product line.
- *Proper exemplars.* If people are promoted and rewarded for non-desired behaviors, then those will become the exemplar behaviors, despite the training.
- *Empowerment.* The employees should have the ability to make decisions to alter and improve their behaviors, as conditions warrant. They should know the "playing field" on which they are responsible for taking action and where the "out of bounds" markers are.

Adults learn in approximately the same way, irrespective of culture and background. Cognitive skills and execution work in certain common patterns. Make that pattern—this sequence—the cornerstone of your training and development, and you'll create that rare combination of effective classroom training which becomes actual changed behavior on the job.

Ultimata: Training is noble work. But performance is the ultimate work. The latter can exist without the former; the former should never exist without the latter resulting.

EMBRACING THE BOSS

I've found that one of the most critical elements in educating any population is educating the boss. The attitude of "Do as I say, not as I do" is alive and well throughout corporate America. The causes vary: sloth, narcissism, arrogance, detachment, ignorance. The result is always the same: failure.

Establishing the learning objectives and adhering to a sequence of adult learning are important, but ultimately futile, if the key exemplar is not, well, exemplifying. Here's how to make that happen.

We had heard disturbing news from the pilot as we approached Washington's National Airport. There were indications that our nose wheel would not lock in place, and we had to jettison fuel and then make a landing at Dulles, where emergency equipment was better able to handle us.

"But as luck would have it," said the pilot in that pilot voice of calm and "right stuff," "I was in the training simulator just last week practicing a landing without a functional nose wheel, so we'll be fine."

"What a lucky break!" exclaimed the woman next to me.

I didn't have the heart to explain that the pilot was more a master psychologist than a master lander with lack of nose wheel. The mere notion that he had been recently trained in a very difficult procedure was enough to comfort her.

Training—even the perception of training—has tremendous power.

For the purposes of my example, "the boss" is anyone managing people who have been targeted to undergo systemic training. The boss is not solely the economic buyer who is funding the initiative, since that person may be far removed with little daily visibility. I'm referring here to every key manager (and, perhaps, supervisor) who manages people being trained.

The Boss's Role in Institutionalizing Learning (as Helped Along by the Consultant)

Number 1. The boss must understand and commit to the purpose of the training. This is not an event being created simply to "get a ticket stamped" on the way to a better job. This is rather a *process* that will create better performance, which will be observable and measurable. Rather than say, "Get back from that waste-of-time training program as soon as you can," the boss should say, "Here are the job accountabilities I want you to focus on during the training, and plan to meet with me when you return to establish an implementation plan."

In most cases, an individual goes to a training program without any inter-action with the boss at all and no connection with what's to be applied, what to expect, and so on. Ideally, the boss should:

- Contribute to the objectives for the program
- Review the program and help to customize it to local need and culture
- Go through the training before the employees
- Create, with the consultants, a plan for using the learning back on the job
- Create metrics to establish effectiveness and fine-tuning requirements

Number 2. The boss should meet pre- and post-session with the participants. Before the program, the boss should explain what's about to happen, review any pre-session materials, help with preparation (reports, case studies, and so on), and indicate how the learning should be applied to priority work concerns.

Subsequent to the program, the boss should review the experience to learn how participants have grasped the concepts, build a plan for application and improvement, and establish review dates to assess progress. *If training doesn't result in improved job performance and results which ultimately reach the customer (including internal customers), then the training is irrelevant.*

Note: This is not a focus on whether the participants *liked* the training. Some of the best courses are created to make participants uncomfortable, chal-lenge conventional wisdom, and change set patterns of behavior. Similarly, *lik-ing* the instructor is not important, and the ubiquitous "smile sheets" that sample the food, temperature, audiovisuals, and other peripheral aspects of training are a waste of time. The only true measure is whether people have actu-ally learned something that can be translated to better performance. (See our discussion of metrics in the next section.)

Number 3. The boss must assist the employees in actually applying the new learning. Sending people who have learned Latin into a Greek-speaking world will ultimately erode the Latin. The job environment's distractions include cus-tomer demands, other departments, existing systems and procedures, col-leagues not yet trained, and other hurdles which can make application of learning difficult.

The boss must change procedures and raise expectations accordingly. For example, if a new set of questions, sales tools, rebuttals, and solutions have been offered to a customer service center, the boss must listen to calls to ensure that they're being employed. Job aids should be created if the course hasn't provided them, e.g., a laminated sheet of objections and rebuttals posted at each work station. Unless the boss actively supports and assesses the training impact back on the job, very little training will actually adhere to the job environment.

Ultimata: A supportive boss can make relatively minor training into an important job enhancement. An unsupportive boss can undermine the finest and most expensive training ever developed. Never overlook the immediate managers. These are the "feasibility" people who will ultimately determine success or failure by their action or lack of action.

Number 4. Finally, the boss must be responsible for providing his or her boss with an assessment of the impact of the training. If this accountability is thrust downward and demanded at set intervals, the boss will have no option other than to examine what's actually happening on the job. And knowing that peers are doing the same things, the boss will also realize that inattention on his or her part might reflect, not on the training—if it's effective elsewhere—but instead on his or her support of that training and its implementation.

If that sounds like blackmail, so be it, but I prefer to consider it to be a strong "embrace." This is a novel notion for many organizations and even for many consultants, but the accountability for measuring impact of training on the job must lie with the front-line manager, who is, after all, in the best position to support the implementation and assess its impact. That simple dynamic also tends to gain much higher commitment (and not merely compliance) from these critical resources.

Ultimata: Never implement a training program when the key sponsors and supporters see it as simply "lip service" or a way to quiet the mobs at the gates. It will fail and you will be blamed. There are no exceptions to this rule.

There was an insurance company in New York City called AIG, which I had been trying to penetrate for a year as a consultant for a major training company. Finally, I was introduced to the vice president of human resources, who occupied a corner office in a fortress-like building close to Wall Street.

I was doing my level best to convince him of line involvement, objectives-based curricula, mutually established metrics, and all the rest, but his eyes just kept gazing out at the East River. Finally, he pointed over my shoulder to a huge grid on the back wall. It was one of those metal charts covering about twenty-five square feet, with magnetic labels running both horizontally and vertically.

"See that, kid?" he asked. "The labels across the top are courses and the labels down the side are key managers" (about thirty of the former and one hundred of the latter). "The more checks I can put on that grid, the more successful I am. If I filled the entire thing, so that every manager went to every course this year, I'd be a hero."

"But how would you know if they were successful using what they'd learned?"

"I don't think you get it. As long as my grid is filled, I've been successful. I don't really care about what goes on after that."

Training is a process, not an event, which occurs normally as depicted in Figure 7.2. While the arrow at the bottom is the shortest distance between the two points of "need" and "results," you must climb up the left-hand side in order to create the downhill slope on the right.

The rather direct line from "need identified" to "results attained" is actually a longer route—the "process"—which has an uphill side and a downhill side.

The uphill side is the preparation required to ensure the success of the training itself, and the downhill side is the implementation required to ensure the results on the job. According to the American Society for Training and Development (ASTD), the annual expenditures on training in the United States alone *excluding travel and related costs* are approximately $60 billion. You are not

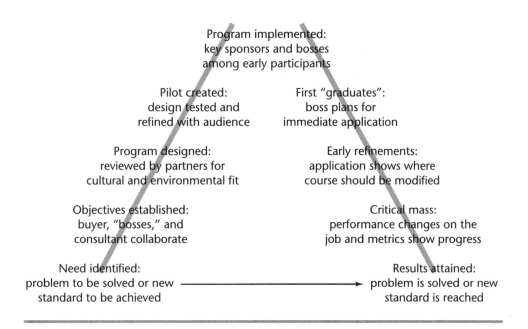

Program implemented:
key sponsors and bosses
among early participants

Pilot created:
design tested and
refined with audience

First "graduates":
boss plans for
immediate application

Program designed:
reviewed by partners for
cultural and environmental fit

Early refinements:
application shows where
course should be modified

Objectives established:
buyer, "bosses," and
consultant collaborate

Critical mass:
performance changes on the
job and metrics show progress

Need identified:
problem to be solved or new
standard to be achieved

Results attained:
problem is solved or new
standard is reached

Figure 7.2. Training as a Process, Not as an Event

reading a typographical error. That's *sixty billion dollars,* most of which is *never justified in terms of return on that investment.* In fact, the training community (human resource professionals, training vendors) has frequently taken the position that "It's just not that important to measure it, because we all know it works."

I've got news for everyone: It mostly doesn't work—first, because the above sequence is seldom adhered to, and second, because the training community has always been loath to examine real metrics of success.

TRUE METRICS
(AND THERE AIN'T FOUR LEVELS)

Over a quarter century ago I heard human resource people talking about "four levels" of measurement, as if it were a basic life force, like wind or fire. I was amazed at what was underlying it.

A university professor by the name of Don Kirkpatrick had written that training could be measured in four areas:

- *Attitude,* meaning that the way people regarded situations had changed and could be measured by survey or interview
- *Knowledge,* meaning that the individuals' competence or expertise was enhanced and could be measured by testing
- *Behavior,* meaning that people were acting differently in the workplace, which could be measured through observation
- *Results,* which meant that performance had actually improved, productivity had increased, errors had been reduced, and so on, measurable by normal indices of job output (e.g., error rates and sales results)

Ultimata: You know you're not with the true buyer when the question you're asked is, "What level of measurement are you going to use?" The correct response to that question by the consultant is, "Take me to your leader."

The only criterion that matters, of course, is results. An attitude shift means nothing if behavior is unaffected. Knowledge acquisition means nothing if it's not applied. Even behavior change isn't always significant if it doesn't lead to desired outcomes. (For example, I may actually see more prospects and make better sales pitches, but if I still don't close business, it just doesn't matter. Science fiction author Stanislaw Lem once asked, "Is it really progress if we teach a cannibal to use a knife and fork?")

When one prepares psychometric testing, there are three primary areas of validation by which to judge a test's potential efficacy:

- *Construct validity:* Was the test created in a manner which ensures non-bias, accurate measurement, and a prevention of "accidental" positives or negatives?
- *Content validity:* Does the test actually measure what it purports to measure, and is there a correlation with actual performance requirements?
- *Concurrent validity:* Do people who perform well now reflect that on the test (or, conversely, do high scorers outperform low scorers)?

Instructional training should be no different:

- Have you created training in a manner which makes it equally effective across cultural, age, gender, and other demographic lines?
- Does the training actually provide skills for the need expressed?
- After training, do graduates perform better than non-graduates?

These are questions rigorously applied by psychologists in testing instruments (and many popular instruments today are simply non-validated "horoscopes" and little more), but not applied at all by the training community. The cyclical trend to abandon even an intent to measure is simply a capitulation to the fact that the training, human resource, and supporting communities are intent on selling product, input, experience, and task, irrespective of the lack of clearly attributable results.[2]

Ultimata: If you insist on training metrics as the consultant, you will make yourself more valuable, enable yourself to create the indices of your own success, and do the client a tremendous service. There is no downside to that combination.

I believe you should focus on the following metrics with every buyer with whom you are proposing a training program of any sort.

Quantifiable, Objective Measures
- Return on investment, sales, assets, equity, and so on
- Sales or profit increases
- Retention of employees or clients (or reduction in attrition)

---

2. Our pop culture exacerbates this. Tony Robbins' popular walks over hot coals have never reflected a proven ability to perform better in the workplace, nor do the "outdoor experiences," which have people forging rivers and rappelling down mountains. It feels good for the moment. So do sugar donuts. But there is no nutrition, and the longer-term effects are actually deleterious.

- Improved market share
- Faster time to market and product cycle times
- Improvement in quality and reduction in defects or errors
- Improved speed and/or accuracy
- Less "failure work" with the problem solved the first time
- Cost reduction
- Waste reduction
- Faster customer responsiveness
- Greater repeat business

Qualitative, Subjective Measures
- Higher morale
- Better communications
- Improved image or repute
- Increased safety

CASE STUDY #28

A division general manager wanted me to train his store personnel to create a "better customer experience." Since the customers were diverse and the stores had varied departments, I wanted to know specifically how he'd know that customers were having a "better experience"!

He then rattled off: "There would be fewer complaints on my voice mail and in my email and in my in-box; the average size of the sale would increase; more people would sign up for our store credit card while onsite; peripheral services, such as the coffee shop and beauty salon, would experience an increase in business; the customer suggestion boxes would receive more comments because people who care are not apathetic; employees would be praised by name and brought to my attention; store promotions would be better supported."

"You've thought about this," I said, shocked. "How did you arrive at all that?"

"Every day for three weeks I trailed customers to the door and asked them what would create a better experience and how might I know it. This consulting stuff is really easy."

- Improved aesthetics or beauty
- Improved comfort or feelings of security
- Increased cross-functional collaboration
- Improved teamwork
- Higher commitment and loyalty
- Greater job satisfaction
- Improved career planning and succession management
- Higher degrees of participation
- Enhanced candor and honest feedback

I'm not saying that you can't measure the second group, because you and the client should, indeed, agree on how you'll know it's present. For example, "greater teamwork" could be reflected in the boss spending less time settling "turf wars" and people voluntarily sharing resources with colleagues. Both sets of metrics are fine, but they require a variety of indicators.

The key is, they are *all* results-focused. Improve those metrics and you'll improve the operation in tangible, demonstrable, readily identifiable ways.

Ultimata: If you can't measure it, you can't prove it's happening, and even if it is happening, you can't prove that you had anything to do with it or that it wouldn't have happened anyway. Put your metrics in place in every implementation—especially training—on one level only: outright results for the business.

FINAL THOUGHT

Never take the easy road, which many buyers are all too willing to allow you to do. When you fall into the swamp, the buyer won't be there to haul you out. Build your own road, with the right materials, on high ground. There will be no question that you built it and that it's the best way to travel.

CHAPTER 8

Developing Client Strategy

If One Has No Port in Mind, No Wind Is a Good Wind

My bias has always been that strategy formulation and implementation are two of the most valuable methodologies to bring to any client. Strategy is important in every operation, from General Electric to the local police department, and it is generally misunderstood by everyone from the local police chief to senior management at GE.

Moreover, working with senior people on strategy immediately conveys two important consulting elements:

1. You are perceived as highly valuable, since you are assisting with the very nature, values, and direction of the enterprise.
2. You will gain ready access to the opportunity for further work: implementing the strategy, working with subsidiaries and divisions, aligning the strategy with the reward system, and so on.

Let's be clear on one important point: I'm talking here about consultants who actually assist in the strategic process by offering alternatives, generating information and analyses, resolving conflicting goals, helping to examine competitive thrusts, and so on. I'm *not* talking about mere facilitation of a strategy retreat or session. The former may encompass the latter, but the latter alone, while helpful, is not remotely as valuable as the former.

The trouble, of course, is that many facilitators are charging more for running such sessions than some consultants are charging for actually actively engaging in the strategy process! And it is a *process*. Strategy is no more established and ready to be executed in a two-day event than is a game ready to be won merely because you've identified and assembled some of the equipment. Someone has to use the equipment, be coached, play by the rules, and use judgment to win the game.

THE FALLACY OF PLANNING

I think the term "strategic planning" is an oxymoron. The confusion of these two terms by executives generally means that both strategy and planning are either nonexistent or poorly executed.

Read twenty books on strategy and you'll find thirty-two definitions of what it is. So here are a few working definitions for our purposes:

> *Strategy* is the act of creating a cogent vision of the future that serves as a template for the decisions made throughout the enterprise which guide the organization.[1]
>
> *Tactics* are the decisions which determine the best options to execute the strategy in order to reach that future vision.
>
> *Planning* is the act of organizing the tactics to ensure quality, timeliness, and efficiency of execution.

Strategy is about the future; tactics and planning are about today. Tactics are about the effectiveness of implementing strategy; planning is about the efficiency of those tactics.

---

1. Ben Tregoe and John Zimmerman have one of the best definitions: "Strategy is a framework within which decisions are made which established the nature and direction of the business." (*Top Management Strategy: What It Is and How It Works.* New York: Simon & Schuster, 1980.)

Ultimata: This may be heresy, but the planning I've seen is always tactical. It's about doing something at a certain time in a certain manner and ensuring that someone is accountable. It is never strategic. It's about ensuring that tactics don't trip over each other.

An example:

The *strategy* of the Inque Ink, Inc., might include the penetration of the overall writing implements, high-end market so that it is the brand of choice among affluent, visible business people and celebrities.

The *strategy* of Apple Computer might include providing the undisputed, preeminent platform for graphics design and illustration.

The *tactics* of Inque Ink, Inc., might include the visible identification of pens when the President signs bills into law and when key contracts are consummated with world-class athletes and sponsors.

The *tactics* of Apple Computer might include convincing the Rhode Island School of Design and the Fashion Institute of New York and the American Institute of Architects to use Apple products at upcoming conventions or exhibitions.

The *planning* of Inque Ink, Inc., would have to include contacting their congressional delegation to lobby for their pens to be used by the President and to contact public relations firms and sports agents to gain access to those managing the contracts and press coverage.

The *planning* of Apple Computer would have to include reaching out to the president or executive director (or finding a friendly board member) of those institutions and to begin negotiating for exclusive use of Apple platforms.

In the planning phases, specific people would be assigned accountabilities, be allocated resources, and be expected to show a certain amount of progress by a certain date. The tactics required to reach the strategic goal may be myriad; and planning around the tactics is required to organize, control, and assure progress.

Planning is a management tool to support strategy, which is an executive tool. Planning, taken alone or as the starting point, will kill strategy as surely as my dog kills that part of the lawn each morning that he uses for his bathroom break. Planning is a ground-up strategy, full of the restrictions imposed by any approach seeking detail, minutiae, efficiency, and micromanagement. Strategy is a top-down approach that creates a vision of the future that the organization is expected to use as its North Star.

Ultimata: If you begin with planning, you will never arrive at a strategy, because planning is based on where you are, not on where you ought to be. If your dream is to live on the water, you don't begin the process by examining how far you can drag your current house.

Figure 8.1 shows the difference between strategy and planning as the starting point.

If you're going to do strategy work at all, you must have your own conceptual house in order. And whether you use my definitions or other definitions, you must be able to clearly articulate to your client how the strategic pieces "fit" and relate to other elements.

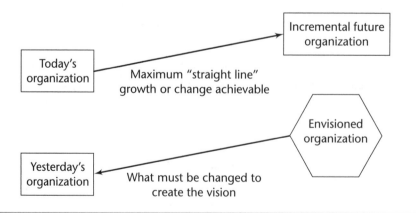

Figure 8.1. Incremental vs. Visionary Growth

On that note, three more quick definitions of what Claude Rains as the inspector in *Casablanca* called "the usual suspects":

Values are the basis for strategy formulation. That is, no organization exists merely to perpetuate itself (I know that's counterintuitive). Merck & Company has a value system that calls for utilizing the best in scientific research and applying it to improving human health. FedEx seems to embrace the value that it provides guaranteed, dependable, and speedy delivery of important items around the world. Ritz-Carlton says that its employees are "ladies and gentlemen serving ladies and gentlemen." (Companies with lengthy values statements often have very poor strategies, as if saying "We respect our employees and believe in diversity" is sufficient to determine their future state.)

Vision is nothing more than an expression of the values and/or strategy of the company in a compact statement. It's often used interchangeably with *mission.* It is often worthless. Saying that "We will become the highest quality ink supplier in the world" is useless unless we know what that means and how we'll know it (and, more importantly, how the customer will know it).

Mission has never meant much at all to me, but often is expressed in a cute "war phrase," such as when Toyota had everyone chanting "Beat Benz" (the launch of Lexus) or Kamatsu invoked "Eat Cat" (meaning their arch-rival, Caterpillar Tractor). These can tend to focus people (would this windshield assembly beat Benz?), but they are often little more than banners in the cafeteria.

Ultimata: Cute phrases and pithy slogans don't change behavior. Aligning people's objectives behind corporate objectives and supporting that behavior with metrics and rewards will usually gain their attention. Rapidly.

If you're going to engage in strategy work at all:

1. Have clear definitions of what the elements are and how they interrelate.
2. Have a clear process for how the executive team is to tackle its role and how managers are to tackle theirs (formulation versus implementation).
3. Hold people's feet to the fire. No strategy fails in the lofty atmosphere of formulation and flip charts tacked to the walls. It fails on the ground, in implementation, while people trample it on their way to fight fires.

THE NOTION OF MOTIVE FORCE

One of the most direct and compelling methods of setting strategy is to help the client determine what the motive force is and what it should be.[2] In fact, if you want to quickly impress a client with the need for your help or the efficacy of your approach, a quick, sharp arrow like this is far superior to dropping the entire edifice of your methodology on the client's head.

CASE STUDY #29

I was knee-deep in what looked like a promising strategy process for a large New York bank when some of the senior vice presidents started what was to be a regular mantra: "They won't let us." Now, I'm used to that in the field or on the assembly line, but not in the executive suite.

"WHO won't let you?" I demanded. After all, the CEO was sitting three feet away.

The guys would pull in their horns for the moment, but periodically, "they" would emerge as spectral eminences in the background. We actually wound up with a relatively tame strategy, not much of a stretch, and far less than the bank might have tried to reach for.

A couple of years later, the bank was acquired and that entire team disappeared. I guess "they" finally did get to them.

---

2. Tregoe and Zimmerman call this a "driving force," but I like "motive" because it denotes both the need for propulsion and motivation. (See *Top Management Strategy,* noted earlier.)

Process Consulting

The motive force is that strategic element which is paramount and propels the business forward. All businesses (all organizations and enterprises of any kind) are in movement. Some are consciously propelling themselves, others are in a default mode, and still others are simply drifting, subject to the vagaries of the tides and the winds. When you drift, you can never guarantee a food source. When your direction is from a default setting you don't completely understand or anticipate, then you're chronically unprepared for the next location.

> *Ultimata:* No organization is at rest. The inertia is to stay in motion, since customers, markets, economies, technology, and other factors are never static. If you are in motion, it's better to have the motor on and a hand on the wheel. Oh, yes, and a profitable destination and a map would also be nice.

The motive force, then, is a particularly lucrative, desirable, competitive, or other strength that the organization now possesses or wishes to develop in order to reach its desired future.[3] If the desired state is the intended port, then the motive force is the engine.

I doubt that there is a definitive list of motive forces, but here are some examples to make the point, since everyone needs a "ten reasons" list.

1. Products or Services Offered. An example would be Boeing, which sells airframes. It is not going to go into the rental car business, even though it could probably afford to buy Hertz tomorrow. And while it may offer a lucrative consulting service and repair capability, those are ancillary to the thrust of the business: airframes. Movie chains sell a service: access to entertainment in the form

---

3. This isn't intended as a book or even a chapter on strategy, but rather one on how best to implement a strategic process as a consultant. If you want to read more about an actual process, see my book *Best Laid Plans*, published by Summit Consulting Group, Inc., originally titled *Making It Work* (HarperCollins, 1996). There are also resources in Appendix B. But please note that this is far more than the insipid and simplistic "SWOT" (strengths, weaknesses, opportunities, threats) analyses that ought to get any consultant thrown out on the street.

of cinema. The proliferation of cafes and the high price of food in the theaters notwithstanding, the chains are there to lure people to the picture show. The rest is peripheral; otherwise they'd be in the restaurant business showing pictures as a sideline in certain rooms.

2. Markets Served. Gillette is in the men's toiletry market. Revlon is in the women's cosmetics market. Some insurance companies and banks, which used to be product and service driven, have changed the motive force (with varying success) to the financial services market. (So instead of being "propelled" by insurance services, they design and acquire new products to meet more of a diversity of financial and investment needs, a very different allocation of resources and image.)

3. Technology. DuPont and 3M are largely propelled by what their scientists and labs produce, which is why you hear about so many "accidental" discoveries that have become products, from Scotchgard™ to Post-it™ Notes. I believe Intel would be in this category.

4. Resources. Kennecott Copper was driven by how much copper it could find and mine, and Weyerhauser is driven by land under forestation. Oil exploration would be counted here. One of my favorites is the old Penn Central, which finally abandoned its railroad but became highly profitable managing the real estate it had all around the tracks.

5. Production Processes. Old-time steel is propelled by the vast investment in physical plant and will lower product prices rather than close plants. I once worked for a training firm actually driven by its capability to print and assemble boxes of materials.

Ultimata: Ask the prospect what the firm's motive force is or, better, ask the executive team. The diversity of answers or glazed looks is all the ammunition you'll need to demonstrate that even the jellyfish are passing by with more discipline and intent.

6. Customers and User Groups. Many trade and professional associations are driven by what their members require, so they may be providing everything from educational offerings and lobbying of Congress to discount insurance and centralized legal help. Amazon.com interests me because they're seen as technology-driven, but I see them as more and more customer-driven (Internet savvy purchaser), as they are offering a wider and wider array of products and services, from collectibles to auctions. eBay may be a customer-driven enterprise at the moment.

7. Method of Purchase. A catalog operation such as Hammacher Schlemmer will place anything in their catalogs—from sprinklers to helicopters—that can be sold in a catalog and ordered by phone or fax. Their retail stores have been a questionable and minor diversion from their real motive force, which is selling anything that an upscale buyer can appreciate in a four-color catalog.

8. Method of Distribution. This, to my mind, is McDonald's, which has increased its food offerings from burgers and fries to salads and breakfasts—anything it can prepare and sell through its food distribution network. (This is different from method of purchase, above, since no one goes into a McDonald's to browse. The buying decision is made prior to entering the store.)

9. Expansion. This is a transient motive force, used to gain image, repute, market share, and/or positioning in either turbulent markets or markets dominated by competitors. Ergo, cable companies, cell phone companies, and long distance companies maniacally have attempted to build customer bases, even at a loss. (When I look at Amazon.com's habitual lack of profit, assuming this was their initial motive force, I begin to wonder about my use of the word "transient"!)

10. Profit. This is the illusory motive force, and that's why I've saved it for last. While most people (and most consultants?) may think organizations are driven by profit, they actually are not from a motive standpoint. Merck doesn't buy Ben & Jerry's Homemade Inc., and Microsoft will not go into the pharmaceutical or liquor businesses. Everyone wants to make money (and non-profits want to save it), but it is only done as a subordination to the actual motive force and strategy. The exceptions are the old-time conglomerates, such as Gulf &

Western and Transamerica, which would own anything from bakeries to insurance companies to make a profit, and the current GE, which owns locomotive companies and light bulb companies, and where the strategy has been to be number one or two in every market.

Ultimata: If strategy does not embrace a top team determining its motive force and how to harness it, then I think the engine has been left at the dock.

CASE STUDY #30

The founder and owner of a $50 million manufacturing business told me at a cocktail party that he was proud that he had never read a management book, never needed a consultant, and was content to have been profit-driven all of his life.

"What's your profitability like over the past several years?" I ventured.

"Well, we're doing about 5 percent, net after tax."

"Really? Well my advice as a consultant would be to liquidate your business, put the proceeds into bonds or other conservative instruments, and you'll create a net of close to 8 percent."

"Are you mad?!" he shouted. "I intend this place to become the leader in liquid control manufacturing in ten years, grossing a half-billion, even if I have to go into hock to do it!"

"Well, then you ought to realize that you're not going to get there pretending that you're driven by profit. You won't make the right investment decisions, and you won't use the correct criteria to judge your success."

"Do you think you're so smart because you've read those books I don't?"

"No, because I write them."

Use whatever mechanism you prefer, but the creation of strategy, aside from clarity, also requires a profound understanding and appreciation of what drives the business and of how the executives control the drive.

THE HUGE ADVANTAGE OF OPTIONAL FUTURES

There are scores of fine methods to assist clients in arriving at a cogent strategy. The problem, however, is that if we are to be more than mere facilitators we must be substantive contributors to content as well as process. That requires business acumen and guts. And it also requires post-heroic consulting.

Our role is to assist the client in examining a range of future states. The present state and its extrapolation shouldn't comprise the future direction by default (or else all you have is a planning process and limited growth). I've found that the best way to help the client to create the most desirable future state is through a choice of options, or alternative futures.

> *Ultimata:* Clients tend to ask, "What should I do?" Our question in response should be, "Here are your options. Which one is most attractive in terms of risk and reward?"

STRATEGIC PROFILING

So the key to developing client strategy is to broaden the client's focus until all possible options—and their likely upsides and downsides—can be methodically and analytically examined. There is no royal road to that scenario, but here is a model (Figure 8.2) I first created about ten years ago and which I've also applied quite successfully to consulting clients. I call it "strategic profiling."

Every business has three customer interactions:

- *Products,* which are purchased tangibles (car or toaster)
- *Services,* which are purchased intangibles (warranty or advice)
- *Relationships,* which are "free" intangibles (trust, exceptions granted)

Strategic Profiling

	Competitive (maintains competitiveness)	Distinct (gains competitive edge)	Breakthrough (achieves dominance)
Product (tangible purchase)			
Service (intangible purchase)			
Relationship (intangible non-purchase)			

Figure 8.2. Developing Optional Futures Through Strategic Profiling

These exist in three dimensions (within any economic strata):

- *Competitive*, undistinguishable from the competition (gasoline)
- *Distinct*, having distinguishing characteristics (one store accepts credit cards, another does not)
- *Breakthrough*, on the leading edge (German-manufactured binoculars or top sports equipment)

By providing any model like this for the client, it's possible to plot the current state (we're not competitive in product and service, but are distinct in our relationships) and the desired future state (stay competitive in product, but move service to distinct and relationships to breakthrough). In my model the gravity is always right to left, meaning that a breakthrough such as anti-lock brakes or air bags in the product category quickly moves to distinct and, ultimately, to competitive.

This means that organizations must constantly improvise and innovate *just to maintain their current position* and must intensely focus on innovation in order to move to the right. Moreover, it's much less expensive to move to the right in relationships (changes in behavior and procedure) than in product (capital investment and restructuring).

Ultimata: The point of a strategic *process* is to create objective and rational decision making and to mitigate emotionalism, turf wars, and subjective analyses. It is also the key bridge to implementation without which nothing happens anyway.

You can readily apply my grid to your own business and begin asking yourself where you are, where you ought to be, and what changes you will have to make in your resource allocation to get there. It's addictive and it's fun, and it will focus your clients on the facts not on the feelings. Whether you use my model or any other, *for implementation purposes* I think you can see the value of applying a process to the engagement and neither winging the proceedings nor applying a simplistic formula to the issues.

If you're going to work in the lucrative field of strategy, here are the implementation criteria which should account for your success and the client's success:

- Utilize a process that engages the client in objective analysis
- Offer both process and content help
- Make sure that the client can completely support the desired state and will accept accountability
- Make sure that the journey from the present state to the future state is clear and that the client understands the support and investment required
- Create implementation metrics and accountabilities

THE TRANSITION TO IMPLEMENTATION

I've never seen a strategy fail in the formulation stages. In fact, they are all spectacularly successful, entombed in three-ring binders with colored tabs, and produced at expensive resorts with fine wine lists.

Strategies fail in their implementation. That's because the following conditions have not been established by the organization or by the consultant:

- Strategy must be translated into operational objectives
- Individual objectives must be aligned with those operational objectives and the strategy they represent
- Accountability must be thrust down to front-line management to ensure performance is supporting those objectives
- Periodic progress must be assessed against established metrics so that fine-tuning can be performed

Ultimata: Strategy should be an organic process, guiding the organization as it, itself, is modified by changing conditions and unexpected developments. If strategy is a static document dusted off once a year for review, it might as well be in the book with the elevator inspection certificates. At least people are testing the elevators every day.

Strategy formulation and implementation, no matter what models you choose to use, coexist as depicted in Figure 8.3.

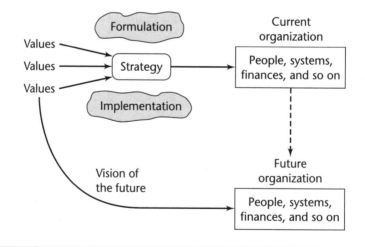

Figure 8.3. Strategy Formulation and Implementation

CASE STUDY #31

An executive vice president of Lincoln Life had brought me in to help him, two peers, and the president work through their strategy. On one occasion, I thought that they were as far along as necessary, were engaging in circular conversations, and making no further progress. I was also watching the clock, because I could still catch a six o'clock flight home.

At about three in the afternoon, the president was wavering, even though his three subordinates seemed content with where they were. Abruptly he turned to me and said, "Well, what do you think?"

"I think we've got it," I offered. "We can work out the details when we're scheduled to meet again on implementation. There's some ambiguity here, but that's to be expected."

"Well, I don't think we're there yet," he said with finality, and we labored on into the evening and reached a point where he was happy. He was also correct. If he didn't have closure, then how supportive could he be of the strategy that was created?

I should have kept my mouth shut about my opinions and simply replied to him, "What I think isn't the issue because I don't have to implement and support this. What's your level of comfort, and where do we need to provide more information and accountability?"

It seems so easy looking back.

Values drive strategy, creating a picture or vision of the future organization. The implementation is designed to manage the existing organization toward that future vision. In other words, the current operation—people, finances, service, systems, rewards, and so on—must be managed into the future operation, meaning that rewards may have to change, the nature of staff may have to be altered, customer service may have to be improved, and so forth (according to the movement required by the model in Figure 8.2, for example).

Otherwise, the current organization may just drift along as it is or move to the upper left or anywhere else, but not in the direction of our vision.

> *Ultimata:* Strategy implementation is the act of managing the current organization so that it evolves into the desired organization. Even though the future state may be a moving target, the point is to head in the same general direction. If strategy is the fuel for change, implementation is the rudder.

If you want to set yourself above the competition in the strategic arena, demonstrate to your prospects how you focus on the transition from strategy *formulation* to strategy *implementation.* Any client who has experienced a poor strategic process or a failed strategic initiative (meaning most of them) will be immediately attentive.

CASE STUDY #32

I had been hired by an insurance company that was having trouble "finalizing" its strategy. It turned out that the CEO had a mantra of "values/vision/mission," which he insisted be examined at weekly operational meetings. Just to make matters worse, or perhaps to have some perverted fun, his subordinates had begun a debate on the differences among goals, objectives, tactics, and emphasis areas. The place was trapped in its own underwear.

After listening to forty-five minutes of incessant debate on definitions, I had had it and really didn't care if they threw me out the window (where I'd probably land on the last three consultants to soften my fall).

"Look," I said, "there are just two items here of interest. Goals (or objectives or outcomes or results or whatever) are what you must achieve for success. Tactics (or tasks or inputs or critical missions or whatever) are the routes that will get you there. This group should agree on the corporate goals; then each department head is responsible for his or her tactics to meet those goals. Now give me the marker."

We were done within the hour.

FINAL THOUGHT

You're really not equipped to help with strategy if your own strategic house isn't in order, even if you're a solo practitioner. What is the desired future state of your business compared with where you are today, and what must you do to get there?

CHAPTER 9

Creating Change

Is Change Management an Oxymoron?

Some things are eternal in consulting, such as sales skills, communication improvement, and effective leadership. Perhaps the overarching granddaddy of constant need is change management.

After all, we all engage in it. Consultants are either requested to create desired change (innovation) or to foil undesired change (problem solving). Yet change management is like the weather. We all talk about it continually, but not many of us seem to do much about it. At consulting conferences everyone nods meaningfully and talks about change management in hushed and religious tones, but that's because actual work in the field has often been more like a religious plea than a cogent consulting approach.

This chapter is about creating change: innovation, initiative, impulse. My philosophy about change (as summarized in Chapter 5) is based on the simple fact that there are only three change agents, and two of them don't work:

1. *Power.* While management can hold the "gun" of money, travel, relocation, perquisites, and recognition to employees' heads, there are two problems. First, this gets movement and not intrinsic motivation so that, when the gun is perceived to have disappeared, so does the desired behavioral change. Second, consultants have no power, nor should they ever be so armed.

2. *Peer pressure.* This is "normative change" in psychological circles and means that people are drawn to behave like their colleagues, which explains why bankers usually look exactly alike, right down to facial hair (on the men). Peer pressure is fickle and can change in an instant. Just ask people who bought Nehru jackets or midi-skirts. Peer pressure, too, results in mere movement. Consultants cannot exert peer pressure except, perhaps, with other consultants, and we're not even very good at that.

3. *Rational self-interest.* When people perceive personal benefit, they tend to change *and to perpetuate the change themselves, which is the difference between motivation and movement.* None of us can motivate others, but consultants can help to establish environments in which people are much more likely to be motivated.

Ultimata: If change is in my best interests, I'll help to lead it. If I perceive change not to be in my best interests, I'll ignore it. If I think change is *against* my best interests, I'll fight it. What perceptions are you creating within your clients?

CREATING AND APPLYING IMPLEMENTATION MODELS

The best way to implement large scale change efforts is to utilize a model which enables accountabilities to be assigned, progress measured, and self-interest realized. There is no perfect model, and Appendix B provides a plethora of sources and change expertise.

An amazingly simple change model is shown in Figure 9.1.

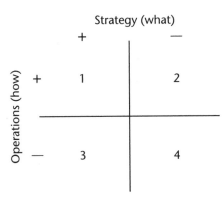

Figure 9.1. A Rudimentary Change Model

In this two-axis chart, the client can help to identify the organization's current state (e.g., strong on strategy and weak on tactics, the converse, and so on). The desired state is already clear: strong strategy and strong tactics. If the client occupies (most likely) Quadrant 2, 3, or 4, the change initiative must focus on the appropriate directions: improving tactical ability, improving strategic thinking, or both.[1] If the client already occupies Quadrant 1, then the change management challenge is to implement techniques to remain there despite changing environments, economies, technologies, demographics, and so on.

Another simple but slightly more sophisticated approach is found in Figure 8.2 in the prior chapter. The "strategic profiling" model also allows for current state, future state, and required change, but in more detail among products, services, and relationships.[2]

No matter how simple or sophisticated a model you use (and I prefer simple), here are the five key steps to implement successful change projects.

---

1. Chrysler under Lee Iaccoca actually moved diagonally from Quadrant 4 to Quadrant 1. Continental Airlines under Gordon Bethune did the same thing.

2. I call these simple templates "process visuals." For an explanation of fifty of them as they apply to all aspects of consulting, see my book *The Great Big Book of Process Visuals, or Give Me a Double Axis Chart and I Can Rule the World* (Summit Consulting Group, Inc., 2000). Also see a sampling of them in Appendix A.

1. Define the Current State.　If you begin with faulty premises or flawed information, your starting point will be on quicksand. Make sure that you and the client are confident of the current state to be changed. *Example:* It currently requires an average of six months and an expenditure of $15,000 to bring a new customer on board. That cost of acquisition exceeds industry averages.

2. Define the Future State.　Create a clear goal that is both a valid "stretch" but also a pragmatic reality. Be careful about "reach exceeding grasp" or you may create an environment in which people are "never successful enough." There must be small victories. *Example:* The goal is an average of four months and $9,000 for average new business that would lead the industry, but only by about 5 percent over competitors. Further, the introduction of new technology should allow for dramatic gains.

Ultimata: The content of the change is the primary responsibility of the client. Safeguarding the process of the change is the primary responsibility of the consultant. When these roles are abandoned—or reversed—the only change is a descent into darkness.

3. Determine Key Sponsors and Implementers.　Who will be responsible for exemplifying and endorsing the change, and whose self-interest must be appealed to in order to implement it successfully? *Example:* The sales vice president and three directors must lead the initiative, and the salespeople in the United States must adapt the new procedures and technology to accelerate the business.

4. Adjust Environment, Feedback, and Rewards to Support Desired Change.　Banners in the cafeteria do not change behavior, and money will change it only temporarily. It's the consultant's job to find and appeal to the rational self-interest that will support the desired change. *Example:* Create a pilot using the new technology and secure endorsement from peers; pay higher commissions on business secured earlier in the cycle; begin a "best practices" weekly meeting to share the best acceleration ideas; provide poorer performance evaluations to salespeople taking longest to land business.

5. Review Progress Against Metrics with Management.   One of the greatest weaknesses of change efforts is that they aren't crisply measured with isolated variables and objective indicators. It's as important to show implementers the progress as it is to show your buyer. *Example:* Provide reports on decreasing elapsed closing times; circulate anecdotal examples of costs removed from sales process (e.g., phone follow-up instead of personal follow-up, use of email instead of visits); dramatize savings and show amortization of technology investment.

ESTABLISHING ACCOUNTABILITIES

Of the five steps above, establishing accountabilities is the most critical. That's because change can only really be led internally, and only by people who lead it through *their own enlightened self-interest.* Organizational change, therefore, even in complex and huge enterprises, is nothing more elaborate than identifying and influencing the relatively few key people who can actually propose, endorse, exemplify, and enforce change.

Ultimata: If you want to change the direction of an aircraft carrier, you don't get out and start pushing. You learn that you have to allow yourself enough room, compensate for momentum, and simply alter a few controls on the bridge. It's the people at those controls who are key.

Most change efforts fail, or at least flounder. It's actually not the mass of people whom you approach or try to influence; it's the small number of people with their hands on the controls. These vital change agents are often people in these jobs or capacities:

- Hierarchical leaders directly in charge of the areas affected. The generals have to lead this charge on their horses from the front, not from a control room at the rear.

- Front-line management, which actually controls day-to-day operations. They are the ones enforcing or not enforcing the new procedures at the point of use.
- Union leaders who may be skeptical of anything proposed by management or by an outsider.
- Respected leaders and experts, whom others regard as objective, interested in the best practices, and successful in their work.

If you can align these four groups (three if there is no union) behind your initiative, you're in very solid shape. But neutral is as bad as negative, since the default position for everyone else will always be the old behavior. You must have these key people *actively engaged* on behalf of your plans.

At the outset of any change process, immediately after agreement with the buyer, identify and "recruit" these key positions. Use the buyer's clout if you must. The most crucial factor in organizational change occurs prior to implementation: It's the conceptual agreement and acknowledged self-interest among the few people who actually have their hands on the controls. The faster the ship has been going, the more delicate and careful (and patient) maneuvering is necessary to change course. Ironically, if the ship is dead in the water, it's easiest to change direction.

Ultimata: Don't be anxious to "make change." If you have a six-month window, for example, invest at least the first month or more aligning your support and key sponsors and establishing their accountabilities. The more time you take with critical sponsors, the faster you will ultimately create change.

CHANGE AS REACTION

Before moving on, let's discuss change models that are quite effective when you're called in not to improve, but to "fix." Figure 9.2 shows a model that is both remedial and more complex at first glance than those above.

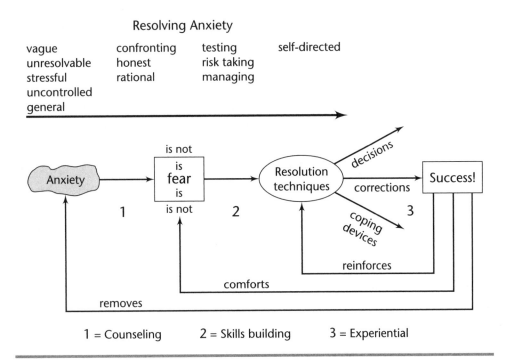

Figure 9.2. A Remedial Change Model

When you are faced with a non-specific problem (communication is poor, morale is low, the environment is low energy, we have no "drive," and so on), don't attempt to deal with what I call "generalized anxiety." That is an amorphous mess and requires the distillation of whatever is really causing the fear. If the client is concerned about the new business plan, is it because of the recruiting needs, the move into Europe, the requirement for new technology, or the matrix structure demanded? In other words, what is the specific fear that is generating the anxiety?[3]

Once the fear is acknowledged (the new technology will cost us months of distraction), the consultant can suggest resolution techniques: Make a decision to shorten the learning curve, correct the problem that causes such

---

3. I consider myself a corporate therapist, and one of my favorite quotes is that "therapy is merely taking a general discomfort and turning it into stark raving fear."

training confusion, or cope with the investment needed by focusing on business growth elsewhere. Those resolution devices should lead to the success that will reinforce their use, comfort the fear, and remove the generalized anxiety.

As consultants, we should understand that moving from general unhappiness to specific fear is a counseling process; moving from fear to resolution techniques is a skills building process; and moving from the skills to actual success is an experiential process. *We must be aware of the point at which we are entering that continuum in order to suggest the proper approaches and recruit the proper support.*

Don't immediately employ skills building (a common "off-the-shelf" approach of poor consultants) when there is still generalized anxiety, and don't attempt to move to successful experiences without the correct skills in place. Whether we use this model or any other, we need to impose a coherent structure around remedial change no less than around innovative change.

Ultimata: Models "frame" the issues so that they are constantly in focus and can be seen on a single screen. They need not be complex nor convoluted, but they should enable you and the buyer to see the picture from a common perspective and focus.

STICKING TO THE BUYER LIKE GLUE

Consultants often implement successful projects in change management at the expense of losing future business. That's because, amidst all the change, the buyer tends to get lost!

During any change management effort, despite size or duration, the following safeguards must be in place to guarantee current success and prepare for future success:

- *Hold regular meetings with the buyer.* Suggestion: Once a week during the first month, twice a month thereafter.

My retail client told me that, despite her personal and emphatic support for better customer service and higher quality staff interactions, her random inspections showed that customers were not being greeted promptly and often had to search for sales help. Moreover, customers were seldom offered additional products and services, and the sales help continued to operate solely as order takers on the floor.

When I investigated, I found that the department managers were under tremendous pressure to keep inventories lean and to report detailed statistics every day to the executives. Therefore, they insisted that the sales help constantly monitor inventories, reconcile discrepancies between sales and returns, and ensure that the paperwork was perfect at the end of every day.

The self-interests of the front-line management were much more aligned toward statistics than service. We fixed the problem by correcting the expectations and rewards and assigning all the paperwork to the accounting department.

I was almost embarrassed to accept my fee, but I managed.

- *Report good news and share credit.* Suggestion: Highlight what's happening well and raise problems within that context. Don't make buyer meetings into "problem sessions."
- *Document progress at key junctures.* As much as I despise written reports, change management projects are too complex to go undocumented. Suggestion: An email summary at least monthly to buyer and key sponsors. Consider hard copy if that better suits the organizational culture.
- *Apprise implementers and other stakeholders of progress.* Suggestion: An electronic newsletter is easiest and best; keep to a single screen with highlights of the project's progress; be honest about setbacks; encourage comment and response; if possible, include a message from the buyer. Weekly newsletters, if brief, are very effective.
- *Use "hotline" or other response mechanisms.* Suggestion: Provide a phone "hotline" option or an email location, or run focus groups and interviews.

(In major projects you can do all of the above.) Seek out patterns in the feedback that show a consistent threat or opportunity. Use this feedback to debrief with the buyer during regular meetings and in the newsletter to demonstrate that people are being heard. The most important thing is to show that you're listening.

- *Solicit ideas and reactions from the buyer and key sponsors.* Suggestion: Ask for a brief amount of time at regular operational or executive committee meetings specifically to provide a quick update and elicit comments. Make sure that no one can say, "I knew that would probably foul things up, but no one ever asked my opinion." You cannot over-communicate with key people during these projects.

Ultimata: Think of the fourth sale first. This project is important, but your long-term relationship with the organization and the buyer is paramount. Don't "disappear" thinking that the project is going well and doesn't require continuing interaction with the buyer. Remember that you're partners, and partners work in tandem.

One of the tremendous fringe benefits of a successful project is a testimonial letter that you can use with prospective clients. The time to establish the basis for that accolade is during these frequent communications and interactions with the buyer. The more you interact, the more closely tied you will be with the results. The less you are visible, the more that it may be assumed that someone else was largely accountable, that your help was peripheral or temporary, or that the changes would have occurred with or without your intervention.

OVERCOMING THE TOUGH RESISTANCE FACTORS

There are some extraordinarily tough, thorny, and potentially poisonous obstacles that arise during change management efforts. These are not the garden variety sloth or apathy, but the entrenched and obstinate barriers. Here are some of the most pernicious, with suggestions about what to do about them.

Resistance: Key sponsors give you lip service endorsement or support, but do not deliver.

Identification: Despite promises and quick agreements, the timing is never right, the resources aren't yet available, follow-up messages aren't returned.

Preventive Action: At the outset, obtain the buyer's approval along with that of the key sponsors for immediate access on a reciprocal basis. Put accountabilities in writing, and ask for progress at common meetings in front of the buyer.

Contingent Action: (1) Take your case to the buyer if the sponsor is critical to overall success and ask for a three-way meeting. Use fact, not supposition (e.g., "He has not changed the sales quota system by the deadline agreed," not "He's just not a team player and is being super-cautious."); (2) If he or she is not critical to overall success, bypass the resistor like an island and flow around. Create your victories elsewhere so that the holdout will be obvious to all and all will be forced to comply.

Resistance: Conflicting priorities are undermining the change effort.

Identification: People are "under the gun" to take care of some important customers, implement a new system, correct an inventory mess, and so forth.

Preventive Action: Create a project schedule and agenda that people have on their calendars so that the work and accountabilities have their own priority and you're not going to people ad hoc with requests that suffer because of other priorities.

Contingent Action: (1) Ask the buyer for a clear statement of the project's priority; (2) Demonstrate that the project's progress will prevent the other "crises" in the future; (3) If legitimate higher priorities do demand the resources and time you had been counting on, bide your time but make it clear to the buyer that the deadlines may have to be moved and you may have to recover lost momentum.

Ultimata: I've never seen a change management project proceed exactly as planned. Stay light on your feet and apprise the buyer that there are bound to be some surprises. If you're close to the buyer, you can weather almost any change. If you're not close to the buyer, a minor change in the wind can capsize you.

Resistance: A real and legitimate failure causes everyone to hit the emergency brake. The client's customers might be complaining, software might be incompatible, or vital people may resign rather than conform to a new procedure.

Identification: People are scared, the buyer is calling you at home, and the critics are now saying, "I told you so."

Preventive Action: There is none. Fortunately, this scenario is rare. Unfortunately, it can be deadly.

Contingent Action: Calmly analyze the nature of the problem. Was it caused by real or perceived failures (e.g., Is the software failing to record some purchases, or are customers simply worried because there wasn't an immediate acknowledgement?)? Shut down all activity on the project for a finite period (e.g., forty-eight hours) while calm is restored and you can provide factual reports. Don't panic, because everyone else is taking care of that emotion. Don't find blame; find cause, which will make people more willing to help you arrive at a solution.

EXPLOITING OPPORTUNITY, OR HOW TO CREATE REVERSE SCOPE CREEP

Change management projects provide the greatest opportunities to create additional business. There is nothing immoral, illegal, or unethical about identifying and pursuing additional business opportunities while working with a client. *The key is to understand and believe that you are providing additional value in new areas for a respected partner and not selling something to an unwitting client.*[4]

In essence, we're trying to create "reverse scope creep," in that instead of trying to confine the client to the parameters of the current project objectives, we're seeking to encourage the client to look at additional value propositions that might naturally flow from the existing relationship and/or existing project.

---

4. See my fourth book in The Ultimate Consultant series, *How to Acquire Clients,* for detailed discussions of expanding existing business.

A high-tech client had a consulting operation in which it had invested zillions. But the consultants were exclusively technological and could talk to other techies, but not to businesspeople. The client wanted a more consultative sales force so that higher margin business solutions could be sold.

When we engaged in videotaped role plays, I often posed as a real buyer who said to the team, "I think we need exactly what you're offering. How do we get started?" Apparently, the opportunity was too overwhelming, because the teams invariably said they'd like to work with my subordinates to do a needs analysis and develop a plan. (The teams demanded later that I burn all of the videotapes.)

Once you've got the buyer, never let him or her go. Hang on for dear life. Hang on for the duration of a project, right into the next one.

Ultimata: The worst time to build repeat business is after a project is completed and you're gone from sight and site. There is an inverse proportion between distance from a successful implementation and ease of selling additional projects.

Reverse scope creep can be accomplished by means of these and related techniques during change management projects:

- *Suggest methods to reinforce desired behaviors far down the road.* Always frame them so that the client can do them self-sufficiently, but also leave the option open for you to assist.
- *Listen to peripheral and tangential conversations that occur with the buyer and key sponsors.* Offer your opinions and even tentative solutions. Encourage them to undertake them independently, but make it clear that you're happy to help if needed.

- *In your general work, make observations about the environment that will be important to the buyer, and report them during your normal buyer interactions.* For example, you might comment on how the buyer's phone is unanswered for long periods of time, or the cafeteria lines require long lunch breaks, or the customer complaints seem to be increasing at the call center.
- *Develop relationships with key sponsors, other buyers, and important recommenders.* Provide them with value during the course of your current project. Always be prepared to help in some manner.
- *Overtly offer.* There's nothing wrong with the following statement: "I know that you're concerned about the haphazard interviewing process, and I thought you might appreciate a proposal on how I would correct the problem. I could easily take it on while working on the supervisory training project and can do it quite reasonably since I'm on site regularly anyway. I just wanted to let you know I do have the competency and capacity if you're interested." What's the worst that can happen?

Figure 9.3 shows that any problem has a cause, which is itself a problem, which has its own cause, and so forth. I call this dynamic "stair stepping."

As the consultant, you rarely enter this chain at the beginning (the "root" cause) or at the end (the superficial symptom). Additionally, since any one level on the stair steps can have multiple symptoms, removing any one cause might or might not remove the entire problem. By viewing cause and effect sequentially like this, you can see that additional projects for the client actually make

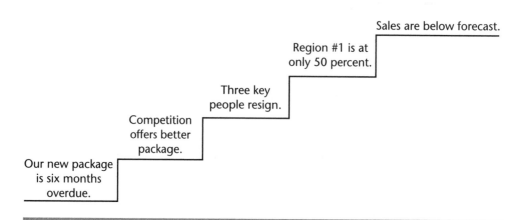

Figure 9.3. Stair Stepping Phenomenon in Project Work

sense. In the illustration, speeding up the time-to-market of the product offerings may remove everything above or may not have an impact on the resignation problem.

Since the cost of acquisition has already been absorbed and repeat business always has a higher margin than new business, every attempt should be made to increase the opportunities within a client system while you are working there.

Ultimata: This is a relationship business. If the buyer trusts you, your suggestions about increased business collaboration will be seen as an attempt to help and as mutual benefit, not as unilateral benefit.

Another way of viewing this dynamic between consultant and buyer is to view both penetration and utility, where penetration is the degree to which your services and approaches are in use throughout the client system, and utility is the degree to which they are acknowledged to be effective and of high value. This concept is graphically displayed in Figure 9.4.

When penetration and utility are both high, there is tremendous client loyalty and trust. When utility is high but penetration is low, the consultant suffers from lost opportunity. He or she can be of very high value, but isn't being sufficiently called on or utilized.

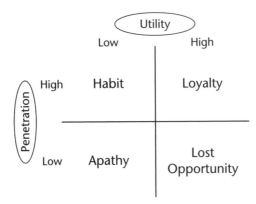

Figure 9.4. Another Way to View Penetration and Utility

When penetration is high but utility is low, the client simply buys out of habit.[5] And when both penetration and utility are low, it's an apathetic situation at best.

Ultimata: Exploit every additional business opportunity that you can. If you don't, no one else will do it for you. As long as you can demonstrate that the buyer and the client are well-served, any project suggestion is ethical and valuable.

While you're creating change for the client, create some change for yourself. Change management projects are the ideal opportunities to establish long-term, high-profile relationships. Another phrase for them is win/win.

SOME THOUGHTS ON TEAM BUILDING

Team building is a rather amorphous area which attracts everything from the "touchy-feely" brigade of "What kind of tree do I remind you of?" to the analytical masters with matrices and elaborate models.

I've included some thoughts here, since I think teamwork is a *byproduct and not a discrete intent.* That is, organization development efforts can build teams, but teams (just like participation) are not always nirvana.

Most organizations that have asked me to work with them on team building actually have committees.

For example, in Figure 9.5, the group on the top, comprising finance, operations, manufacturing, sales, marketing, and R&D, can either hit or miss their goals. They might cooperate and collaborate under mutually beneficial circum-

---

5. I once worked for a training company that would annually sell a quarter million dollars worth of pre-packaged training to the likes of IBM and Kodak. Neither company could demonstrate any ROI on the investment, but had long since established the habit of middle managers having their "ticket stamped" through attendance at these workshops. My boss said, "Hey, don't rock the boat with these kind of sales." But I always wondered how much more work we could have done at high prices if our utility were more clearly understood.

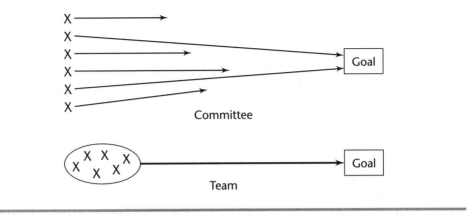

Figure 9.5. Individual vs. Team Efforts

stances, but there is no imperative for, say, sales, to sacrifice resources, power, or prestige to manufacturing. They can go it on their own. These are committee heads (or medieval fiefdoms) at work.

In the bottom dynamic of the figure, they either all make the goal or all fail to make the goal. In this case, sales had better surrender some budget to manufacturing if the latter needs to retool unexpectedly, because without everyone pulling his or her weight, no one crosses the finish line.

Make no mistake: Most organizations run with committees (silos, turf, departments, whatever the euphemism) and not true teams. *You can't develop teamwork in a committee.* That's why I'm relegating team building to a subset of organizational change efforts. It's not an end in itself, and some very successful organizations have fostered internal competition (e.g., the product rivalry for shelf space within P&G or the sales contests that habitually produce winners and losers).

If it does make sense to build teams, your project needs to address these types of issues:

- Is there common incentive and reward throughout the team?
- Can the team make decisions about key issues, for example, expenditures, hiring, performance evaluations, customer complaints, and so on?
- Does the team have a procedure to air grievances and problems candidly within the team itself?
- Is the team sufficiently heterogeneous to represent its customers, a diversity of values and opinions, and innovative thinking?

For years the training firm I worked for had major clients who were buying for simplicity's sake. The training materials we provided were well-known and effective, despite showing their age. We never tried to develop any relationships with anyone outside of the HR and training departments, and we were really order takers more than anything else.

But as more firms entered the training arena and technology simplified both manufacture and dissemination, prices came under tremendous pressure. We would hold out until the fourth quarter, then start offering deals in order to make our plan. The closer we got to December 31, the better our deals.

Finally, one year my buyer at Honeywell didn't make his usual summer purchase to prepare for fall training. "We're going to use something else to get us through," he said, "then make a larger purchase from you during your annual December fire sale."

That's when I decided that I would someday get out of the box business and into true consulting.

- Is there a structure to determine formal or informal team leadership?
- Are there self-regulating metrics to determine team progress and distance from its goals?

Teamwork and team building are valid means to attain certain ends. I've found that they are virtually never ends in and of themselves and that projects based solely on the objective of "better teamwork" usually either peter out or are deemed unmeasurable.

FINAL THOUGHT

Change management projects, by definition, entail high degrees of ambiguity. Don't insist on rigid order or flawless structure. You're better off with a flexible process that can adjust to changing conditions.

CHAPTER 10

Improving Leadership

The Power Is in the Engine Room, but the Wheel Is on the Bridge

I've saved leadership until the final chapter because I believe it is the most important area in which consultants work. I've seen superb companies destroyed by inept leadership (Apple, before the return of Steven Jobs) and poor performing companies renewed by excellent leadership (Continental Airlines' phoenix-like rise under Gordon Bethune).

Leadership development is the sanctum sanctorum of any organization. If you are able to reach, influence, and improve its leadership capabilities, you'll find that all other problems are quickly resolved and all other opportunities are rapidly exploited. That's because the effective leader, whether CEO, divisional, departmental, or informal:

- Serves as *the* main exemplar of behavior
- Ultimately controls the reward systems
- Chooses the type of people who represent him or her

- Establishes the pragmatic operational values
- Sets the pace of change

There are four main components of consulting on and to leadership that we'll examine: the routine leadership behaviors; the extraordinary leadership behaviors; the recognition of where and when to make tough decisions; and the recognition that quality of leadership is measured not by the leader but by the led.

For any reader who is also leading a firm and employees, this chapter is intended to be read on that basis, as well.

EMPHASIZING RANGE, NOT STYLE

Historically, leaders have derived their power from these four sources:

1. *Hierarchy:* The title on my business card or office door denotes my power. If my card says "vice president of finance," then all lesser titles must do as I request. This is the basic Roman Legion approach, still very much alive in any military operation. Majors don't argue with generals.
2. *The ability to reward and punish:* This is sometimes directly correlated with hierarchy, sometimes not. If a manager in another department, or a customer, or a superior I don't respect and might ignore has the ability to provide or withhold money, job assignments, recognition, freedom, visibility, credit, and so on, I may well be swayed by his or her demands.
3. *Expertise:* I will follow a leader whose competency and information are crucial and which exceed my own. A colleague on our sales team may always be the one to have the final decision on resource allocation if she is the widely accepted authority on how to close complex sales. An underwriter might always sway colleagues and even hierarchical superiors if it is acknowledged that he has never accepted a risk that resulted in a loss for the company. A relatively low-level employee might be the leader in South American expansion if he is the only one who has worked there and who speaks the language.

> *Ultimata:* When leaders order, threaten, or demand, they may create movement. When others willingly want to follow, they have created motivation. Movement is snail-like. Motivation is transformational.

4. *Innate respect:* This is often called "referent power," and it means that I will follow you because I believe in you. This means that I respect and trust you and believe that your decisions are objectively reached and fair to all of us. This is also, however, charismatic leadership, wherein I don't need to carefully evaluate the elements, because if you've decided something, it's good enough for me. Ironically, we complete the loop back to the military, when soldiers charge into withering fire, not because the general orders the charge, but because the general *leads* the charge. The ancient Spartan leadership always fought at the head of their troops in the most dangerous and exposed positions.

Consultants should work toward imbuing leaders with referent power. I'm convinced that the difference between the great organizations and the also-rans is almost entirely influenced by this one factor. Referent leadership doesn't have to be dramatic, "warm and fuzzy," or even overtly charismatic. But if you had to assign a single reason for the success of GE and not Honeywell, Southwest Airlines and not US Air, Dell and not Osborne, HP and not DEC, Chrysler[1] and not GM, the Green Bay Packers and not the Cincinnati Bengals, or the Girl Scouts[2] and not the Boy Scouts at certain junctures of their respective histories, then you'd have to point to the leadership during those times.

Not every leader can be a Jack Welch[3] at GE or a Fred Smith at FedEx, but every leader can embody virtues of clear values (e.g., speed, cross-functional

---

1. Say what you will about Lee Iaccoca before or after, but he nearly single-handedly led Chrysler out of the abyss and toward record profitability.

2. Which no less an authority than Peter Drucker has called the best-managed organization he has ever seen.

collaboration, strong values at GE) and walking the talk (e.g., leading by example, providing ample rewards, keeping the customer first at FedEx).

The consulting "model" here, I believe, is to demonstrate that leaders have behavioral options and that one "style" or approach can't possibly be optimal in a world of diverse conditions and changing times. This is precisely why consultants using (often invalid) personality profiles and behavior labeling tools are doing a huge disservice to their clients. The point isn't to master a "perfect style," but rather to gain success in every situation.

Ultimata: Show me a leader with a single, inflexible style and I'll show you someone with a track record of success that brings new meaning to "lackluster." Leadership is not about personal comfort; it's about organizational success.

The outstanding work in this field has been conducted by Dr. Victor Vroom of Yale University over the past thirty years.[4] He has found that there is a range of behaviors available to the leader which are applicable depending on the variables in the leadership situation. (The descriptions are mine, and no value judgments are intended—all of these behaviors can be highly effective or ineffective, depending on the circumstances.)

Autocratic behavior occurs when the leader makes decisions alone, without any other inputs or inquiries. This may be highly effective when the leader is certain that he or she possesses all necessary information, when others will accept a "leader-alone" decision, and when time is of the essence.

Approaching behavior occurs when the leader seeks bits of information from others but doesn't reveal why (e.g., "What is our attrition rate so far this year?"). This behavior is useful for acquiring vital missing information rapidly and for making decisions when commitment is not required.

---

3. And if you don't believe in organizational change or the impact of changing leadership, just think back to the "neutron Jack" days of GE and compare them with more contemporary times.

4. His original book on the subject, *Leadership and Decision Making* (University of Pittsburgh Press, 1973), was written with Philip Yetton.

Consultative behavior means that the leader talks to people one-on-one, reveals the nature of the decision, and elicits people's opinions, suggestions, opposition, support, and so on. This behavior works well when involvement and participation are needed and time is not critical.

Group behavior occurs when the leader convenes the appropriate group, openly discusses the issue, and encourages spirited debate while retaining the decision-making prerogative. This approach requires time, but also gains commitment and maximum participation while safeguarding against people or groups that may not share the same objectives as the organization (hence, the leader makes the final decision).

Consensus behavior is similar to group behavior, except the leader tells the group that the decision is the group's to make and commits to live by that outcome (and doesn't attempt to directly or indirectly influence the process). This style maximizes ownership and employee development, although it requires the most time.

Vroom's research demonstrates that when a leader chose within a "feasible range" of behaviors, he or she was successful by pre-established standards over 80 percent of the time, but when the leader deliberately chose a style outside of the feasible set, the rate of success was less than 20 percent. (The feasible set premise means, for instance, that if you know you do not have sufficient data, you cannot use the autocratic style; and if you know that the group doesn't share organizational objectives, you cannot use the consensus style. See his book, listed in Appendix B, for the entire research regimen and results.)

Whether you utilize Vroom, another source, or your own construct to develop leadership abilities within your client, the need for a cogent model is again paramount. Referent power is the key leadership factor, and it is best gained through a consistency in approach (not a single style, but an approach to styles) and the successes emanating from that approach.

Ultimata: Leaders are only effective within some context which consultants must help identify and organize. CEO John Scully was a success at Pepsi-Cola but a disaster at Apple because the context changed, but his choice of styles didn't. You cannot develop leadership without understanding context.

Effective leadership development is not simply coaching on a grand level. It's the development of consistent processes and interactions that embrace a multitude of differing factors and changing conditions.

CRISIS MANAGEMENT: THE EXTRAORDINARY

One of the problems entering the new millennium was that over 90 percent of all corporate leaders had never led during bad times. The euphoria of technology during the Nineties covered a multitude of sins, and deficiencies of leadership were glossed over by outstanding earnings reports.

In more turbulent and uncertain times, however, deficiencies in leadership are torpedoes in the bow, and the enterprise flounders badly. If there were an area of consulting deficiency and/or organizational blindness in the Nineties, it was in not using the luxury of good times to help leaders prepare to manage in bad times. Instead, they've been forced to learn rather abruptly.

Airline pilots have two critical events in their flights: takeoff and landing. All the rest is routine and usually handled by automated equipment. A professional speaker faces two vital junctures in addressing the audience: the opening and the closing. Everything in the middle will fall into place nicely if the audience is "hooked" at the outset and convinced of some action at the conclusion.

Leaders spend most of their time on the routine, especially if they've effectively delegated, chosen good people, and empowered the troops. It's the few decisions at crisis points—the takeoffs and landings, openings and closings—which earn them their pay. (My dog could have led most companies during the boom times of the Nineties, since most were simply propelled by the economy and the main idea was "not to screw up.")

Ultimata: Leadership in crisis is not like other aspects of leadership. It is very much alone in the end, but requires continual input along the way. It is the true measure of a leader.

When General George Gordon Meade, commanding the Union Army, faced Robert E. Lee at Gettysburg, he realized that he lacked complete information about the battlefield. He sent an aide, General Gouverneur Kimble Warren, an engineer by trade, on a reconnaissance. Warren rode to the extreme left flank of the Union line and climbed a hill called Little Round Top.

To his abject horror, he looked down to see Confederates wheeling artillery laboriously up the unoccupied hill, from which they would flank the Union position and drive Meade from the field. Scrambling down the hill, he yelled at the first Union officer he found to take his men to the top and hold at all costs. That man was a volunteer, Colonel Joshua Chamberlain, commanding a volunteer regiment, the 20th Maine.

They arrived a scant two minutes prior to the enemy, which had slower going with the artillery pieces. Three times the Confederates charged, and three times they were repulsed. Finally, there were just enough men left and there was just enough light left for one more assault. Except this time, the Confederates ran toward an eerie silence, because the 20th Maine had run out of ammunition.

The men looked at Colonel Chamberlain, half expecting a retreat, since they had done everything humanly possible. Chamberlain looked at the advancing Confederates, then looked at the exposed Union lines and issued one of the great orders in the history of the United States military: He said, "Charge!" and led his men down the other side of the hill.

The remnants of the 20th Maine ran toward the Confederates screaming like banshees. The latter, brave men, made the only rational conclusion possible: These men charging must be fresh troops, and the position had been reinforced. The Confederates retreated, and Little Round Top, the Union lines, and Gettysburg were saved. There are monuments to Warren, Chamberlain, and the 20th Maine on that spot today, and Chamberlain was awarded the Medal of Honor.

Referent leadership at work

In preparing leadership for crisis management, a consultant should include the following discipline, at a minimum:

- Rapid and continual communication to staff and customers
- Clear explanation of when, where, and how decisions will be made
- Crisp decision making without qualification or equivocation
- Personal involvement and visible participation of the leader

When a Merck plant suffered an explosion in Puerto Rico during Roy Vagelos' term as CEO, he immediately cancelled a meeting in California, flew back, went directly to the plant, visited the families of those injured and killed, and personally launched an investigation. Local authorities, the press, Merck employees, and all other interested parties had full and open access. Vagelos later said that he had no "war council" or consulting, but simply immediately did what he thought was right.

During his tenure, Merck was also named "America's Most Admired Company" by the annual *Fortune* magazine poll a record five consecutive times. If anyone can disassociate that accolade from Vagelos' leadership, they must be using mirrors.

The focus during crises must be to eliminate or blast through what I call the "thermal zone," those organizational levels which carry different self-interests in crises: safety, avoiding blame, fear reaction, escape, and so on.[5] The Thermal Zone is illustrated in Figure 10.1.

When Alexander Haig, in that infamous moment after President Reagan had been shot, said to the television cameras, "I'm in charge here," the Thermal Zone was roaring hot, since almost everyone realized that constitutionally he was not in charge and pragmatically he was not in charge. During the Tylenol crisis, CEO Jim Burke obliterated Thermal Zones, while in the *Exxon Valdez* disaster CEO Lawrence Rawl literally disappeared and the Thermal Zone was paramount.

---

5. The Thermal Zone can also exist during non-crises, which is a dead giveaway of poor leadership, never monitoring whether direction and values are being operationalized.

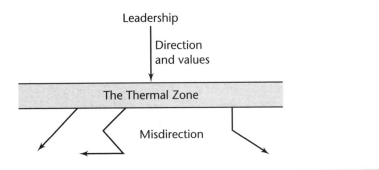

Figure 10.1. The Thermal Zone

Ultimata: Thermal Zones will deflect, divert, and refract leadership if it is weak, vacillating, or uncertain. They are a natural phenomenon of the leaderless, seeking comfort and protection in crises. Superb crisis leadership obliterates Thermal Zones.

TOUGH LOVE VS. "NOT ON MY WATCH"

A chronic weakness of even outstanding leaders is the "savior syndrome." Many executives seem to believe that any person who fails in a job during the leader's regime constitutes a personal failure for the leader.

Throughout my consulting experience I've seen outstanding leaders undone by inferior subordinates *whom they refuse to replace.* This is not contradictory to the maxim that strong people surround themselves with strong people. I believe that leaders tend to appoint and select good, tough subordinates, which is a proactive measure. But at the same time they are weak at removing poor, "soft" subordinates who are already in place, which is a reactive measure. Since consultants are often called in to deal with remedial circumstances, it is precisely those poor performers—the detritus and flotsam of a prior administration—who are encountered in key reporting positions.

As consultants, we can't improve leadership merely by improving a single person. We have to improve the environment and culture—and also the key

When a United Airlines DC 10 lost all hydraulic power in flight some years ago, the cockpit crew acted as a team. The captain listened to the first and second officers provide information, and another captain on board knelt on the floor to help work the controls. That team approach was credited with saving as many lives as possible during a crash landing that would otherwise have been impossible.

In crises, researchers have noted that leadership decisions from a single source are vital, but supported by the willingness to listen to the advice, counsel, and information from a diversity of sources. Research results have also demonstrated that leadership is best supported by heterogeneous teams rather than by homogeneous teams.

Consultants who assist leaders in crisis management must focus on this duality: sole accountability and direction based on a multitude of sources and ideas. This is not a skill which naturally develops in every leader, nor one honed during good times.

Leadership during crises is much rarer than takeoffs and landings, so it must be continually tested and energized, to be ready in the rare cases when it is needed. If you offer that capability as a consultant, you'll be going where few consultants have gone before and vastly enhancing your value.

supporting players. An outstanding leader will do a lot to assist in those other areas, but external intervention is usually also necessary.

We have to invoke a "tough love" approach by pointing the leader to the higher ground. He or she is responsible and accountable for the entire scope of the project, and ultimate performance against goals is far more important to the customers, other employees, and shareholders than is the determination that no one "fails." Moreover, we are doing a poor performer a tremendous favor by realistically assessing his or her performance and removing that person from a job that he or she simply can't do, even if it means termination. (The ultimate adverse effect in not doing this is seen when a customer is told to avoid a certain claims examiner, or service technician, or appraiser *by colleagues in that same workplace.* The poor performer is tolerated but customers are protected by conscientious others, although this casts doubt on the entire operation. Imagine being told not to fly with a certain pilot!)

Ultimata: The law of averages alone would tell you that a small percentage of inept and inappropriate performers are in a variety of jobs in even the best run organizations. It's up to leadership to weed them out and not waste time on development that should be invested in the *top* performers.

This tough love approach is vital for a very pragmatic organizational return on investment. Most organizations spend far more time, money, and attention on poor performers and attempted remedial action than on star performers and commensurate supportive actions. We've all seen it. The best performers are left alone ("It ain't broke, don't fix it") and the laggards receive the best possible developmental resources, which will largely serve as a balm for leadership consciousness that "something ought to be done."

What ought to be done is that people should be removed.

If you're involved in a leadership development effort, think about the following template, which will enable you to stand out in a crowd:

- Establish and pursue developmental goals for the leader.
- Assess the leader's direct reports and create a "triage" ranking:

  1. Superb people who should receive more support and latitude
  2. Potentially superb people who can develop into position number 1 and require mentoring and targeted development
  3. Poor performers who should receive clear performance expectations and deadlines within which to meet them

- Work with the leader to allocate resources and the leader's attention accordingly. The goal should be to eliminate position number 3 by either moving people to position number 2 or removing them altogether.
- Assess the direct reports of the people in position number 3. There is a good chance that they have received no development, are themselves poor

performers, and/or there might be a position number 1 person ready to be moved up as a replacement.

This kind of exercise can be done annually. Every organization I've ever seen is better served by leaders who invest in improving their best performers rather than by investing vast resources in trying to "save" poor performers.

Leadership is about making tough calls, not about being loved. It's about allowing the best and brightest to take the lead by weeding out the snags and entanglements of those who would drag their feet.

Ultimata: Leaders can be tough, be loved, and be effective, like Herb Kelleher at Southwest Airlines. Or they can be tough, unloved, and effective, like Jack Welch at GE. Or they can be tough, unloved, and ineffective, like Al Dunlap at Sunbeam (and every other place he's been). The point is that leaders who surround themselves with excellent people whom they hold accountable will almost always be sensationally effective.

The priority in organizations used to be: (1) shareholders, (2) senior management, (3) employees, (4) customers. More recently, that sequence has been reversed: Take care of the customers and the employees will benefit (fewer complaints, better working conditions, easier to do the job); if the employees are doing well, senior management can focus on key priorities (because turnover is low, decisions are being made at lower levels, actions are consistent with strategy); when senior management is focused, the shareholders are treated very well (effective management of assets, high margin returns, new markets entered).

In this quarter-to-quarter world, with executives sweating out the next board or executive committee meeting, the smart consultants are nonetheless focusing their clients on customers, service, and relationships of the business. Those are the keys to the second sequence noted above.

Leadership has to come from the front, not the rear. And it must be based not on the cult of the leaders and infallibility, but on empowering and leveraging the total talent of the organization. In a sense, this kind of leadership is "post-heroic."

The CEO of a $400 million division asked me to work with his vice president of strategy, who was not performing well and had a series of interpersonal problems with his peers. Over a thirty-day period, I found the man to be deceitful (promising actions but never taking them), attempting to degrade colleagues, trying to set up a "we versus them" attitude with his staff, and generating constant excuses for why the strategy was taking so long. (I suspected, correctly, that he knew virtually nothing about strategy, but had fast-talked himself into virtually every job he'd ever held.)

I reported to the CEO that there was nothing to be done, and that the vice president should be fired. The CEO implored me to spend another thirty days, saying that the fee was unimportant. He had to try to help this guy "on his watch."

During the second thirty days, I was confrontive. While the vice president told me he understood the gravity of the situation, he quickly began trying to undermine me with the CEO and other executives, which was entirely predictable.

At the end of that thirty-day period, the CEO asked for another extension ("Let's at least give it an entire quarter"). I told him that I couldn't do it and, further, that if the Board ever knew how much of his time was being drained by attending to this guy and patching up the problems he caused (by our calculation, about 20 percent of the CEO's total time), rather than being spent on strategy, mergers, new markets, and so on, he'd have a lot of explaining to do.

The guy was fired that week. It was the greatest service I performed for that client.

POST-HEROIC LEADERSHIP AS A CONSULTING OBJECTIVE

I've written elsewhere in this series about "post-heroic consulting," and the same philosophy applies to leadership. The best leadership is by exception, not by routine.

Leaders require a holistic approach to their organizations and account-abilities.

Figure 10.2 shows that external (consultants) and internal (staff functions) resources support both teams and individuals in pursuing the organization's business goals. Nothing occurs in a vacuum. In fact, the dynamic is rather like a hydraulic system—press something in one place, and something else moves in another.

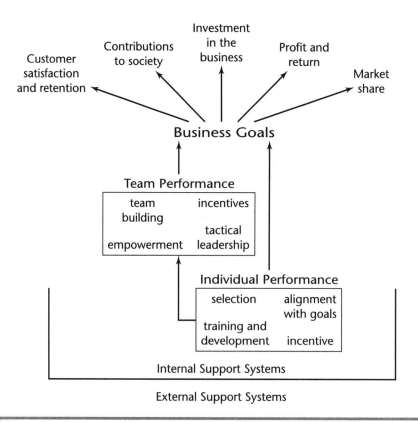

Figure 10.2. A Holistic View of Leadership

I called *The Wall Street Journal* and *Business Week* to place an ad for a client to support a project we were initiating. The woman at *The Wall Street Journal* told me it was an unusual ad, one which she couldn't promise would run, and that she didn't know when she would be able to get back to me, since many people involved were outside of her control. Exasperated, I asked what her job was.

"I take advertising insertion orders," she loftily explained, "and you're not giving me one I can take very easily." My fault.

At *Business Week,* the woman echoed that it was an unusual ad, but then said it was a real challenge, and that she'd assemble a team, get back to me by ten the next morning, and that I shouldn't worry, because "We'll make it work for you."

"Really?!" I said. "And what's your job there?"

Incredulous, she said simply, "I'm paid to improve your business."

Simple as that. Two people making the same salaries, sitting at similar desks, receiving similar perks, in similar environments, but one takes advertising insertion orders—an input—and the other improves my business—an output.

Which leadership would you rather instill and develop? The one that creates the ad taker or the one that creates the business enhancer?

Consulting to leadership requires that the focus be on the business outcomes and that the workings of the system then be arranged and led to ensure the maximization of those outcomes. *That is, post-heroic leaders manage results, not tasks, outcomes, nor inputs.*

Post-heroic leadership focuses on results and outcomes. Consequently, intervening leadership is by exception. Post-heroic leaders don't get nervous if someone isn't at his desk or doesn't answer her phone. They are concerned with results, be they monetary, client satisfaction, safety, or whatever the goals happen to be. These leaders are, by definition, "big picture" and macro thinkers. They are not immersed in minutiae and never micromanage.

> *Ultimata:* When you find someone micromanaging, it is almost always because of a lack of trust. If you don't do the job the way he or she would do it, you must be doing it incorrectly. If the leader has trust in subordinates, simply providing the goals should be sufficient.

Here is my favorite checklist for creating a post-heroic leader.

Ten Ways to Identify the Post-Heroic Leader

1. *The leader must listen carefully and never cut off others' contributions.* Most people are content merely to have their stories heard, even if dramatic action doesn't necessarily follow.
2. *The leader never reacts rashly or abruptly.* Logic rules emotion in terms of interpersonal responses. Anger should virtually never be apparent.
3. *The leader leads by example.* Talk is cheap. The leader's behavior and actions match his or her vision and spoken words.
4. *The leader empowers.* That means simply that people are allowed to make decisions which influence the outcome of their work. Approvals are kept to a minimum.
5. *The leader is accessible.* This means physically—not barricaded behind corporate dining room doors—and emotionally—not intimidating or threatening when approached.
6. *The leader embodies diversity.* There are direct reports, associates, and others in the leader's circle who mirror the larger employee and customer demographics. Conflicting opinions and dissent are welcomed.
7. *The leader creates a clear strategic thrust.* People know why the organization is in business and what their roles are in that business. There is virtually no vacillation.
8. *The leader is innovative.* Prudent risks are taken and setbacks are taken in stride. The antithesis of a risk-averse atmosphere prevails.

> *Ultimata:* What The Ultimate Consultant ideally seeks to create is The Ultimate Leader.

9. *The leader demonstrates the difference between right and wrong.* Ethical considerations are clearly discussed and applied. The operation succeeds by doing what is right, not by doing whatever is necessary.
10. *The leader bestows credit.* The post-heroic leader makes other people into heroes.

Consulting on leadership, I'm convinced, is the most powerful thing we do as consultants. Do it well and the results will rebound to your enduring best interests.

FINAL THOUGHT

Leadership is driven by values and measured by results. If you can successfully convey that to your client, you are in rarified air.

Sample Process Visuals

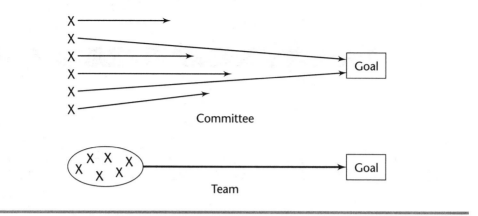

Figure A.1. Individual vs. Team Efforts

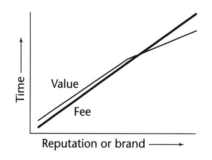

Figure A.2. Fee Follows Value Until Strong Branding Enables Value to Follow Fee

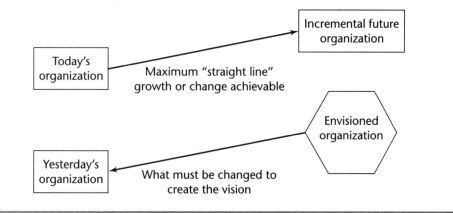

Figure A.3. Incremental vs. Visionary Growth

Figure A.4. The Self-Esteem Cycle

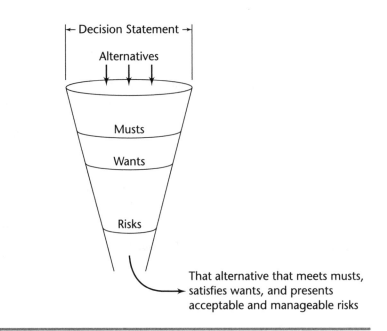

Figure A.5. Decision-Making Funnel

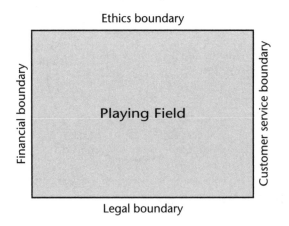

Figure A.6. The Empowered Playing Field

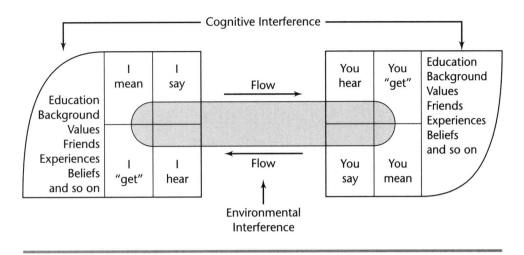

Figure A.7. Communications Flow and Interface

$$\frac{\begin{array}{c}\text{Tangible Outcomes} \times \text{Expected Duration of Outcomes} + \\ \text{Intangible Outcomes} \times \text{Emotional Impact of Intangibles} + \\ \text{Peripheral Benefits} + \text{Variables Positively Affected}\end{array}}{\text{Fixed Investment Required}} = \text{Client's "Good Deal"}$$

Figure A.8. "Good Deal" Equation

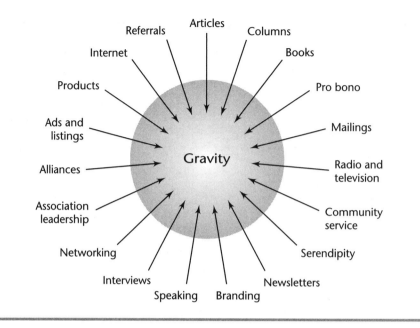

Figure A.9. The Gravity of Marketing Efforts

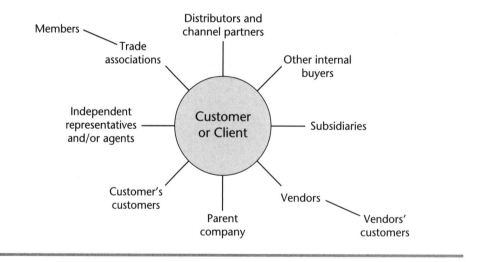

Figure A.10. Finding Lateral Buyers

Annotated Bibliography

Read 'Em All and You'll Be in the Top 5 Percent

You'll note that most of these works are not recent, which is because most of the excellent work was done quite some time ago.

Argyris, Chris. *Integrating the Individual and the Organization.* New York: John Wiley & Sons, 1964.

> A prolific writer and pre-eminent psychologist, Argyris wrote this book on combining positive team building with individual well-being to create improved performance.

Bellman, Geoffrey. *The Consultant's Calling.* San Francisco: Jossey-Bass, 1990.

> One of the outstanding books on consulting you should read. Geoff focuses on the philosophy and values of the profession.

Bennis, Warren, and Nanus, Burt. *The Unconscious Conspiracy.* New York: Amacom, 1976.

> The original and still best work by Bennis on leadership, subtitled, "Why Leaders Can't Lead." Everything else he's done is really a variation of this work and his "leaders are made" philosophy.

Drucker, Peter. *The Changing World of the Executive.* New York: Times Books, 1982.

> One of the master's two best, the other being *The Effective Executive.*

Drucker, Peter. *The Effective Executive.* New York: Harper & Row, 1966.

> The only person who makes my list twice. This is still a powerful work, and probably his best.

Fiedler, Frederick. *A Theory of Leadership Effectiveness.* New York: McGraw-Hill, 1967.

> The champion, perhaps, of the contingency theory approach to leadership.

Gabor, Andrea. *The Capitalist Philosophers.* New York: Times Business, 2000.

> A critically acclaimed set of short biographies on everyone from Mary Parker Follet to Elton Mayo.

Gardner, John. *On Leadership.* New York: The Free Press, 1990.

> Simply one of the best, most succinct writers on the subject.

Gibson, James, et al. *Organizations.* Chicago: BPI/Irwin, 1988.

> A graduate-level, excellent text. Later versions are probably available.

Gilbert, Tom. *Human Competence.* New York: McGraw-Hill, 1978.

> Work carried on by Geary Rummler today. Focuses on the performer as part of a stimulus-response dynamic.

Jay, Antony. *Management and Machiavelli.* New York: Bantam, 1967.

> Enjoyable and lucid discussion of politics and maneuvering in organizational cultures.

Likert, Rensis. *New Patterns of Management.* New York: McGraw-Hill, 1970.
One of the toughest writers to comprehend; nevertheless, his studies on leadership and performance led to some groundbreaking work at the University of Michigan.

Mager, Robert. *The Mager Library.* Belmont, CA: Pitman Learning, 1984.
If you haven't read the collected—and insightfully funny—works of Mager, you aren't educated in this industry.

Maslow, Abraham. *Motivation and Personality.* New York: Harper & Row, 1970.
Classic work on hierarchy of needs and human motivation.

McClelland, David. *Human Motivation.* New York: Scott, Foresman, 1985.
Need/achievement theory and connections to Maslow's work.

McGregor, David. *The Human Side of Enterprise.* New York: McGraw-Hill, 1960.
His classic work on Theory X and Theory Y.

Sampson, Anthony. *The Company Man.* New York: Times Business, 1995.
A good history of companies and organizations and the reasons for their current structure.

Schein, Edgar. *Process Consultation.* Reading, MA: Addison-Wesley, 1969.
Still *the* authority on process consultation.

Schultz, Duane, and Schultz, Sydney Ellen. *Psychology and Industry Today.* New York: Macmillan, 1990.
A graduate-level text that's clear and coherent. This is the fifth edition, and there is probably a newer one available.

Taylor, Frederick Winslow. *Scientific Management.* New York: Harper, 1911.
This is a terrific book by the "first" management consultant. A "must" read if you're serious about the profession.

Tregoe, Benjamin B., and Zimmerman, John. *Top Management Strategy: What It Is and How It Works.* New York, Simon & Schuster, 1980.

> One of the most straightforward discussions of strategy extant; still accurate and useful today.

Vroom, Victor, and Yetton, Philip. *Leadership and Decision Making.* Pittsburgh, PA: University of Pittsburgh Press, 1973.

> More recent work is available, but this is their seminal book on situational leadership. It's tough sledding. Often referred to as "normative" or "path/goal" theory.

Weiss, Alan. *Million Dollar Consulting.* New York: McGraw-Hill, 1992, 1998, 2002.

> You didn't expect this not to be here, did you? Seriously, mine is the only book that focuses on the combination of consulting as a craft *and as a business.*

Zaleznik, Abraham. *The Managerial Mystique.* New York: Harper & Row, 1989.

> One of the most vocal in terms of "leaders are born, not made." A counterpoint to the work of Bennis.

Index

109; on managing unforeseen dramatic
events, 95; on measuring institutional learning, 120; on motive forces, 132; on observational coaching, 57; on post-heroic leadership,
173; on recognizing depression, 69; on rules
of engagement, 60; on sabotage, 101, 102; on
using surveys, 45, 49; on "tough love"
approach, 171; on value of observation, 51
Causes of failure, 102–103
Chamberlain, Joshua, 165
Change agents: overcoming resistance, 83–86;
three factors of change and, 80–81, 142; work
of real, 81–83. *See also* Culture change
Change management: case studies on, 149, 153;
dynamic "stair stepping" and, 154*fig*–155;
overcoming tough resistance factors, 150–156;
reversing scope creep with, 153–154; safeguards with buyers during process of,
148–150; team building and, 156–158. *See also*
Culture change
Change models: remedial, 147*fig*; rudimentary,
143*fig*. *See also* Culture change
Chrysler, 143n.1, 161n.1
Client education checklist: co-opting key sponsors, 4; establishing clear accountabilities, 3–4;
establishing crisp objectives, 3; establishing
metrics, 5; preparing buyer for wins/losses, 5
Client strategy development: creating/applying
implementation models, 142–145; fallacy of
planning and, 124; notion of motive force
and, 128–133; offering optional futures to
client, 133, 134*fig*; strategic profiling and,
133–135; strategy, tactics, and planning elements of, 124–128; transition to implementation, 135–138, 136*fig*; two consulting elements
involved with, 123–124
Clients: defense against scope creep by, 92–94;
five-step checklist for educating, 3–6; offering
optional futures to, 133, 134*fig*; receptivity to
your methodology by, 2; scope creep denial
by, 90–92; strategic profiling of, 133–135;
viewing penetration and value, 155*fig*. *See also*
Buyers
Closure, 17
Coaching key people: establishing rules of
engagement for, 58–61; fourteen warning
signs of personality, emotional, and medical
disorders, 67; observational, 54–58; opinions
regarding, 53–54; providing effective feedback, 61–66; recognizing depression when,
68–69; twenty questions for effective, 60–61;
when more than one coach is required, 66–68.
See also Key players
Cognitive dissonance, 73

Compensation (or reward) system, 84
Concurrent validity, 118
Conducting interviews, 42–43
Confidentiality: observing, 24, 31; rules of
engagement on, 58; walking the tightrope of,
31–34
Conniver, the, 11–12
Consensus behavior, 163
Construct validity, 118
Consultative behavior, 163
Consulting interventions: avoiding environmen-
tal/political land mines during, 10–13; condi-
tions for successful, 1–2; educating the buyer
for successful, 2–6; metrics during, 5, 117–121,
145; role of key players in successful, 6–10;
ten steps to launch, 14–18. *See also* Objectives
Content validity, 118
Continental Airlines, 143n.1
Contingent actions, 151
Crisis management, 164–167
Culture change: benefit in relation to status quo
and, 86*fig*; case studies on, 83, 87; checklist
for, 73–74; cognitive dissonance as foe of, 73;
creating exemplars and avatars for, 74, 76–78;
elements of culture and, 72–74; overcoming
resistance to, 83–86; as reaction, 146–148; rein-
forcing, 79–83; remedial and rudimentary
models of, 143*fig*, 147*fig*; two kinds of, 71–72;
viewing penetration and value of, 155*fig*–156.
See also Behavior; Change agents; Change
management
Customers: considered in strategic profiling of
client, 133–135; as motive force, 131; talking
to the, 24
the cynical and uninformed, 13

D

Darkness Visible: A Descent into Madness (Styron),
68n.4
Data collection. *See* Gathering intelligence
strategies
Depression, 68–69
Dilettante, the, 12–13
Distribution method, 131
Dramatic events: defining key, 94–95; six ways
of controlling chaos from, 96–97
Driving force, 128n.2
Drucker, Peter, 161n.2
Dunlap, Al, 170
DuPont, 130

E

Embracing the boss, 112–117
Emotional disorders warning signs, 67

Empowerment, 112
English China Clays (ECC), 48
Environmental/political land mines, 10–13; the conniver, 11–12; the cynical and uninformed, 13; the dilettante, 12–13; vested interest, 11
Ethical conduct requisites, 33*fig*
Expansion motive force, 131
Expertise power, 160
Exxon Valdez disaster, 166

F

Failure causes, 102–103
Federal Reserve Bank, 93
Federal Reserve Bank of New York, 75
FedEx, 72, 161
Feedback: adult learning sequence and, 110–111; alternating between soft and hard, 63–64; case study on, 64; dedicating personal time for, 62; during implementation, 144; including positives in, 62–63; providing effective, 61–66; providing frequent, 62; rules of engagement on, 58–59; set up monitoring points/progress indicators for, 65–66; supported with examples, 63
Feedback loops, 111–112
"Feel good" sessions, 107
First-name relationships, 27
Focus groups: balance sheet on using, 37–41; case studies on using, 41; focusing, 36; sample letter of participation invitation to, 39; ten steps to successful, 37–40
Fortune magazine, 166
Fourteen warning signs of personality, emotional, and medical disorders, 67

G

Gathering intelligence strategies: Alan's ten methods of, 24–25; to challenge basic premises, 20–23; creating ethical baseline for, 26; establishing alternative sources of information, 23–26; need for, 19–20; rules of thumb for accepting data using, 23
Gathering intelligence tactics: balance sheet on using focus groups, 37–41; conducting interviews, 42–43; creating/implementing surveys, 43–48; focusing a focus group, 36; observation as, 50–51; staffing "hot line," 48–49
GE (General Electric), 161, 170
Gillette, 130
The Great Big Book of Process Visuals, or Give Me a Double Axis Chart and I Can Rule the World (Weiss), 143n.2
The Great Big Book of Process Visuals (Weiss), 7n.2

Group behavior, 163
GTE's corporate university, 109
Gulf & Western, 132

H

Haig, Alexander, 166
Hammacher Schlemmer, 131
"Hawthorne Effect," 50
Hewlett-Packard, 28, 72, 90
Hierarchical power, 160
Holistic view of leadership, 172*fig*
Honeywell, 157
"Hot lines," 48–49
How to Acquire Clients (Weiss), 2n.1
How to Write a Proposal That's Accepted Every Time (Weiss), 2n.1

I

Iacocca, Lee, 143n.1, 161n.1
IBM, 156n.5
Implementation: creating/applying models of, 142–145; establishing accountabilities during, 145–146; transition from strategy to, 135–138, 136*fig*
Incremental vs. visionary growth, 126*fig*
Individual vs. team efforts, 158*fig*
Inertia, 86
Information. *See* Gathering intelligence strategies
Innate respect, 161
Inque Ink, Inc., 125
Institutional learning: case study on measuring, 120; case study on, 113; as process not event, 117*fig*; qualitative, subjective measures of, 120; quantifiable, objective measures of, 119–120; role of boss in, 113–117; sequence of adult, 109–112; setting objectives for, 106–109; true metrics of, 117–121. *See also* Organizations
Interviews, 42–43

J

Jobs, Steve, 10, 159
Joint accountabilities, 14

K

Kamatsu, 127
Kelleher, Herb, 170
Kennecott Copper, 130
Key players: determining who are the, 6, 8; finding and meeting the, 15; implementation role of, 145–146; road map to influencing/educating, 8–9. *See also* Coaching key people; Sponsors

Kirkpatrick, Don, 117
Knowledge, 118
Kodak, 156n.5

L

Leadership and Decision Making (Vroom and Yetton), 162
Leadership development: case study on, 168; crisis management and, 164–167; emphasizing range instead of style, 160–164; holistic view of, 172*fig*; importance of, 159–160; post-heroic objective of, 171–175; The Thermal Zone and, 166–167*fig*; tough love approach to, 167–171
Lee, Robert E., 165
Lem, Stanislaw, 118
"Lemming approach," 80
Lethargy, 86
Lincoln Life, 137
Little Round Top battle (Civil War), 165

M

McCarthy, Eugene, 84
McDonald's, 131
Machiavelli, N., 1
Mager, Bob, 5, 106, 110
Maginot Line of resistance, 84
Making It Work (Weiss), 129n.3
Mallinckrodt, 95
Managing misfortune: major causes of failure, 102–103; sabotage, 97–102; scope creep, 90–94; unforeseen dramatic events, 94–97
Markets served, 130
Meade, George Gordon, 165
Medical disorders warning signs, 67
Mercedes-Benz North America, 17
Merck, 15, 41, 48, 131, 166
Method of distribution, 131
Method of purchase, 131
Metrics: establishing, 5; during implementation, 145; of institutional learning, 117–121
Microsoft, 131
Mid-course corrections, 17–18
Mileposts, 59
Million Dollar Consulting (Weiss), 106
motive forces: case study on, 132; described, 128–129; list of, 129–132
Moving through ambiguous zone of change, 75*fig*

N

Neutral turfs, 28

O

Objectives: establishing crisp, 3; establishing learning outcome, 106–109; establishing mileposts to measure, 59; organizational education tied to strategic, 108*fig*; post-heroic leadership, 171–175. *See also* Consulting interventions
Observation, 50–51
Observational coaching: case study on, 57; checklist for, 56–57; described, 54–56
Optional futures through strategic profiling, 134*fig*
Organizational education/goals link, 108*fig*
Organizations: challenging basic premises of, 20–23; defining current and future state of, 144; eating in cafeteria of, 24; follow dress codes of, 31; holistic approach to, 172; investigating service of, 25–26; making your success visible to, 16; motive force of, 128–133; observing social mores of, 30–31; observing the, 50–51; searching for incongruities for, 25; staffing "hot line" for, 48–49. *See also* Institutional learning

P

Peer pressure as change agent, 80, 142
Penetration and value, 155*fig*–156
Pepsi-Cola, 163
Personality disorders warning signs, 67
Posing, 27
Post-heroic leadership: as consulting objective, 171–173; ten ways to identify, 174–175
Potential problems. *See* Environmental/political land mines
Power: as change agent, 80, 142; sources of leadership, 160–161
Preventive actions, 151
The Prince (Machiavelli), 1
Process visuals, 143n.2
Production processes, 130
Products/services: as motive force, 129–130; strategic profiling using, 133–135
Profit, 131–132
Proper exemplars, 112
Proper reward, 112
Purchase method, 131
"Push back" approach, 20

R

Rains, Claude, 127
Rational self-interest change agent, 80, 142
Rawl, Lawrence, 166